Schwarzenegger Syndrome

Schwarzenegger Syndrome

Politics and Celebrity in the Age of Contempt

Gary Indiana

THE NEW PRESS

NEW YORK
LONDON

© 2005 by Gary Indiana

The excerpt from the speech by Jim Kunstler on page 80 is used with the kind
permission of Jim Kunstler.

Requests for permission to reproduce selections from this book should be mailed to:
Permissions Department, The New Press, 38 Greene Street, New York, NY 10013

Published in the United States by The New Press, New York, 2005
Distributed by W. W. Norton & Company, Inc., New York

The preface of this book originally appeared, in different form, as "Maintenant que les
voeux sont des chevaux, meme les cochons peuvent chevaucher," in *Le Purple Journal,*
No. 3, Vol. 7, 2004.

ISBN 1-56584-951-5 (hc.)
CIP data available

The New Press was established in 1990 as a not-for-profit alternative to the large,
commercial publishing houses currently dominating the book publishing industry.
The New Press operates in the public interest rather than for private gain, and is
committed to publishing, in innovative ways, works of educational, cultural, and
community value that are often deemed insufficiently profitable.

www.thenewpress.com

Composition by Westchester Book Group

Printed in the United States of America

10 9 8 7 6 5 4 3 2 1

For Michael Phipps, and Lily

Einigkeit und Recht und Freiheit
Für das deutsche Vaterland
Danach laßt uns alle streben n
Brüderlich mit Herz und Hand!
Einigkeit und Recht und Freiheit
Sind des Glückes Unterpfland.
Blüh' im Glanze dieses Glückes,
Blühe, deutsches Vaterland.

Brüderlich mit Herz und Hand!
Einigkeit und Recht und Freiheit
Sind des Glückes Unterpfland.
Blüh' im Glanze dieses Glückes,
Blühe, deutsches Vaterland.

(Unity and justice and freedom
for the German fatherland;
This let us all pursue,
Brotherly with heart and hand.
Unity and justice and freedom
Are the pledge of happiness.
Flourish in this blessing's glory,
Flourish, German fatherland.)

Heinrich Hoffmann von Fallersleben, 1841,
"Das Leid der Deutschen"
Melody: Josef Hayden, 1797

Contents

Preface: The Excremental Republic

When the U.S. presidential contest of 2004 began to be widely framed as "the most important election of our lifetimes," a statistically unmeasured number of Americans registered this claim as the stubborn, nostalgic residue of progressivist optimism, an appealing but futile, empirically baseless belief in the indestructible fairness and moral decency of "the American people"—essentialist qualities, thought to be embarrassingly violated by such shockingly un-American phenomena as conspiracy and fraud at banks and energy companies; insider stock trading; piratical trade practices at pharmaceutical corporations, insurance companies, manufacturing conglomerates, and even utility providers; rampant bribery of judges and legislators; revenue-skimming from domestic programs by government appointees; grotesque civil rights abuses; promiscuous use of military force; and deployment of "intelligence services" to overthrow legitimately elected, reform-minded governments in parts of the world considered possible sources of future exploitation.

The official accounts of such lapses, equally firm in the belief that corruption and reckless disregard are un-American, typically lament the "unintended consequences" of tax code loopholes, failure to spot loose cannons in the bureaucratic morass of government agencies, misfiled secret documents, wrongly interpreted telexes, distracting personal emergencies, excessive apprehension on the part of one or another faction of advisors, failure to switch off the office coffee machine before leaving for the weekend, and other circumstances synonymous with "accident."

Note that "unintended" and "accidental" are always the favored constructions. American governments do not make mistakes, hence cannot admit any, and therefore can never learn anything from them. The deepest and most lingering quintessence of this fantasy, the Vietnam War, remains for many Americans, all these decades later, what the Versailles Treaty represented to Germany's extreme right wing during the Weimar Republic. The atrocities Americans committed at My Lai and in countless "strategic hamlets" have been monstrously relativized as "unfortunate incidents" of a type that happened "on both sides." (In this connection, Noam Chomsky has noted that the only war crimes prosecuted at Nuremberg were actions the Allies hadn't also committed themselves—if we do it, it's acceptable warfare; if they do it, it's a crime against humanity.)

While most countries indoctrinate their schoolchildren in exalting national myths, the United States is unique among advanced nations in its cartoonlike educational dogma of America's unblemished history of noble intentions, global altruism, heroic vigilance in pursuit of universal justice. The magnetic allure of its boundless freedoms accounts for the envied magnificence of its economic system and the perfection of its institutions. In short, this farrago of preposterous homilies and infantile clichés constitutes the average American's entire civic education—which, in the absence of credible evidence or any nuanced historical sense, erases fact from the public sphere. It reduces the principle of self-government to a parody of consensus, "elections" that generate no cerebral activity but instead spawn endlessly iterated, meaningless bromides and the touting of numbingly irrelevant "issues" instilling a collective sense of unreality.

From a strictly constitutional perspective, the most important election of our lifetimes was not, in any meaningful sense, an election at all, but the judicial travesty of a per curiam Supreme Court opinion, issued only in written form (traditionally, important rulings are first delivered orally) at ten in the evening on December 12, 2000, which halted the Florida recount and thus awarded the American presidency to George W. Bush.

The ruling itself, for legal scholars and jurists, was an astonishing corruption of judicial practice: "per curiam" is a term applied almost exclusively to unanimous decisions on matters of such untroublesome triviality that the customary written opinions of the individual justices are considered unnecessary. None of the Court's nine justices were identified by name on the December 12 document. Yet the opinion that decided *Bush v. Gore* was far from unanimous, and the issue at stake was one of profound and repercussive national importance.

Moreover, the wording of the *Bush v. Gore* opinion stipulated that the Court's "consideration is limited to the present circumstances, for the problem of equal protection in election processes generally presents many complexities." This caveat, disclaimer, whatever you want to call it, was unique in the history of American and Anglo-Saxon law, and in fact nullified the foundational basis of the entire legal system, which is, of course, the understanding that any ruling by a court, unless reversed on appeal, establishes a precedent to be invoked in subsequent rulings. In the case of the Supreme Court, there is no higher venue for appeal, and hence no possibility of reversal. In effect, it now became the law of the land that one of the Court's most historically controversial decisions immunized itself from becoming the law of the land, on one hand deciding who would occupy the nation's highest office, on the other hand eradicating itself from legal history. The opinion virtually acknowledged its illegality.

It was assumed by media pundits and politicians alike that the fury ignited by the obviously partisan character of *Bush v. Gore*—even taking the case proved the Court majority's bias in favor of Bush—would quickly subside, and recognition of a fait accompli would "unite" Americans in conciliatory acceptance of the new president. For a time, actually, it seemed superfluous to dwell on the new president's illegitimacy, since his manifest incompetence and surpassing ignorance were embarrassingly clear even prior to his swearing-in ceremony. He was, perhaps, the only chief executive in history presumed to be fated for a single term before his inauguration, even by most people who had voted for him.

But, as history teaches us, shit happens.

A week after this mush-mouthed, dyslexic, perpetually vacationing cipher hit an unprecedented nadir of public approval, Condoleezza Rice, conferring with staff a mere twelve hours after the attacks of 9/11, perceived them as a providential "opportunity" for Bush and his administration. The adage that every disaster is someone's stroke of luck is a central article of faith for Ms. Rice, and can equally apply to her government employment vis-à-vis the disaster of Bush's presidency-by-fiat.

The events of 9/11 brought violent death to almost 3,000 people and a chance for George W. Bush to posture like a painfully constipated fire marshal in the London Blitz, costumed as a rescue worker perched atop the smoking wreckage of the World Trade Center, whining a litany of vapid solemnities through a megaphone that seemed surgically implanted in his voice box ever after. His "resolve" to avenge the dead and hunt down "the evildoers" (in more recent Bush Ebonics, "suiciders") who "hate America for its freedoms" moved hearts and marginally sentient minds in every trailer park and industrial bidonville across America. Our country had, after all, suffered a deep wound, and though this wound was only more visually ubiquitous than America's seldom-videotaped, indiscriminate slaughter of civilians—in far greater numbers than the 9/11 fatalities, all over the world, in "conflicts" that never involved actual declarations of war, in promiscuous bombings of select infrastructural targets within sovereign nations, and uncountable violations of international law—the United States squeezed a Niagara of sympathy from much of the world, even from countries it had itself terrorized for entire generations. Having no moral aversion to violence himself, Bush interpreted this sympathy as a global endorsement of his own terrorist agenda.

Declaring a "war on terror" and himself a "war president," Bush instantly reactivated long-standing plans to invade Iraq while intimidating Congress into passing the Patriot Act, a malignant assault on numerous constitutionally guaranteed civil liberties. The Bush administration seized the "opportunity" of 9/11 and the panic it created so adroitly that the administration itself might as well have planned it. The consolidation of power after 9/11 allowed by a president elected with the questionable mandate of fewer than 200 votes bore an eerie resemblance to the political aftermath of the Reichstag Fire.

The "war on terror" facilitated a concurrent war *of* terror on the citizenry, waged with cynically manipulative, fake warnings of imminent attack, the discovery of "sleeper cells" in various backwater communities, proliferation of "security measures" in every conceivable public location, sweeps and arbitrary arrests in certain ethnic neighborhoods, incarcerations—without specific charges, indictments, trials, or right to legal counsel—and harassment of political activists, as well as Nixonian investigations into the private lives of journalists, intellectuals, and dissident entertainment figures. Bush's costume switch from ranch hand overalls to military uniforms from the Homeland Security wardrobe department enabled the presidential hologram to unleash his congenital belligerence, his use of language as a tool of deception, and a view of human existence as a "faith-based," apocalyptic clash between good and evil. Decades of drink and subsequent embrace of religious psychosis made him the ideal transmitter of "values" epitomizing the death instinct. The type of divine guidance Bush asserts at every opportunity lost its totalitarian grip on the Western mind during the fifteenth century. Its recrudescence in twenty-first-century America says less about religious faith or "a personal relationship with Jesus Christ" than it says about a power structure that systematically cripples public education, demonizes the concept of a national health system, flatly denies scientific proof of global warming, considers the poisoning of our air and water insignificant side effects of economic expansion, and jails an aberrantly high percentage of African Americans for victimless crimes as a method of disenfranchisement.

The kill-or-be-killed ethos of contemporary America presents itself as, variously, free trade, healthy competition, individual self-empowerment, liberation from "big government," meritocracy, whatever. Its practical effect is the total dismantling of an already vestigial social safety net; its goals are the erasure of every social welfare program instituted since Franklin D. Roosevelt's New Deal, elimination of Social Security, and the fusion of government with global corporations. The result will be peonage for the vast majority of the population, enslaved to international business entities for the basic necessities of existence; the "securities" provided will be privileges bestowed on disposable servants, instead of rights ensured by the government.

By the final days before the 2004 voting, of course, how much was still at stake had become clear. The poll figures narrowed to a virtual tie, reactivating the calamity of 2000 as portent of something even more crippling to the practice of self-government. This time several states might have thrown the election into chaos. Armies of lawyers were deployed to polling places. Testing of electronic voting machines proved them to be unreliable, defective, and simple to hack into, their memory cards easily removed and replaced with counterfeits. Republican intimidation of black voters proliferated in every state. Election observers from other countries spread through the South and many northern states as well. It was, at last, clear to at least half of America how much damage had been done to the electoral process in 2000, how many of our institutional foundations had been compromised, how little that had seemed immutable, even in the darkest crises of the past, remained.

On the Republican side, the campaign was unquestionably the filthiest and most unscrupulously conducted in American history. The Democratic side made the usual reductive compromises with its largely ceremonial pandering to its supposed "base" of minority citizens and progressives (which it had not served with any credible efficacy even when the Democratic Party held power under Jimmy Carter and Bill Clinton), while both underestimating and overestimating, with astoundingly bad timing, the extent of the public's surrender to reductive catchphrases, buzzwords, perceptual reshaping by television commentators, and primitive opinions drawn from the facial expressions, tones of voice, and body language of politicians, from baseless warnings of imminent catastrophe, from patently false assertions, and so on. The miniaturization of important things into trivia practiced by mass media became the public's imitative reflex. When a verifiable, damning fact emerged—for example, the looting of an unsecured weapons depot in Iraq—the outrage such information once would have generated was deftly refocused on accusations that a proven fact was reported "for political reasons," that its "timing" was suspect. The novel questioning of why news was reported replaced the content of factually reported news.

Another innovation in the media discourse, one I find difficult to elucidate, may have less to do with partisan sparring than the intrinsic inanity and feigned reflectiveness of many American journalists. It appears in opinion columns (and, increasingly, in reportage itself). The columnist, rather than speculating on the meaning or consequences or implications of the reported event, places the event "in context." The event is likened to many other events, often events of the very distant past, or likened to events whose similarity to this event is either specious or superficial. Or the comparison itself reduces to virtual parity a large event and an event of such smaller magnitude that it amounts to saying that an ant and an elephant carry around the same body weight.

This species of opinion writing often involves a deftly insinuated pretense of vast historical knowledge or some other expertise in a highly cerebral activity. A harmless enough fakery in itself, but the actual effect of the column is its assurance to the reader—whose moral, ethical, and intellectual reaction to the news story might otherwise produce alarm, and, cumulatively, among many such readers, civic action—that the news is actually "nothing new." It has happened before. It happens all the time. It will happen again.

At its most ludicrous, this barbecue of something new into nothing new compares a current event of terrifying barbarism with an event, or series of events, that occurred in the era of barbarism that followed the era of savagery and evolved over centuries of agonizing, brave, persistent struggle against brutality and ignorance into civilization. And it is at this ludicrous juncture that the opinion columnist most witlessly collaborates with the trivialization of civilization's regression to barbarism. The inability of a badly educated generation to reason becomes a change of styles, tastes, slang, attitude, etc., a superficial matter that "always happens." An election fraud in 2000 is "nothing new" because "it happened before" a century ago. A loaded gun fired into a person's brain has always been fatal. Lemmings have always thrown themselves off cliffs.

The words "always" and "never" should be closely scrutinized when they appear in political discourse of any kind. Neither is automatically credible, nor often used to tell the truth in modern journalism.

But I am wary about blaming George Bush's 2004 victory on the media, submental political rhetoric, and other mind-softening external forces. Leftist and liberal journalists have the habit of flattering the public's irrationality and abdication of responsibility by citing irresistible, demoralizing influences that render it powerless. Trick us once and you're the fool. Trick us into fooling ourselves and we're idiots. The world is everything that is the case, begins Wittgenstein's *Tractatus Logico-Philosophicus*. If the existence of persistent, principled, rationalist resistance to barbarism ceases to be the case in the time ahead of us, the world will belong to any tyrant who claims it.

Schwarzenegger Syndrome

ONE

Madison Square Garden, August 2004.

Lighting and decor by Albert Speer, perceptual fog machines courtesy of your local cable provider.

The Republican National Convention played out in a militarized hot zone, overlit for optimum frenzy, a spy blimp floating in the summer-doldrum sky, spy cameras garnishing lampposts in red plexi cylinders, a *cordon sanitaire* of New York's Finest and Secret Service agents steadily widening the encircling "perimeter," the instant arrest zone, in the direction of Siberia. Had rumor of chilling new "intelligence" offered a tactical advantage in stretching out the convention an extra week or so, the perimeter would have engorged most of New York City, ranging as far north as 120th Street and way south of the sanitized hole where the World Trade Center towers had once wobbled, with such architecturally brilliant harmlessness, several feet back and forth in a strong breeze.

New York is often more daring than other cities. In Los Angeles, it would be quite remarkable for an apartment building construction site to advertise its future desirability with a wraparound banner of adjectives containing such ominous items as "undulating" and "provocative," as what had once been planned as a Rem Koolhaas hotel in Astor Place was currrently promising. And New York has traditionally absorbed enough urban trauma that the RNC was hardly sophisticated enough to set it undulating for more than a couple of days. A few religious maniacs with box cutters, on the other hand, had rendered a fest of brainless patriotism like the RNC a bit superannuated and unwelcomely "provocative" for an entire generation.

Like the exuberantly xenophobic delegates who wore and waved itty-bitty plastic U.S. flags like medieval plague talismans inside the Garden, protesters had spilled into New York from Everywhere, USA. Parks and churchyards sprouted bicycle-festooned encampments of the cheerfully disgusted young. New Yorkers posted Internet offers of free spare bedrooms and couches or plain floor space to crash on. Some ads screened out smokers and nixed other unwanted habits. In others a distinct craving for any sort of company was legible between the lines. Parts of the city looked like the sixties for a few days, the fun hippy sixties, rather than the demonic caricature conservatives never tired of conjuring as the nadir of American "values."

After everyone left, the Republican mayor genially noted that the protesters had boosted the city's revenue considerably more than the Republican Party had. Weeks before either faction turned up, many New Yorkers questioned the value of any protest. The people who owned the mass media made public demonstrations disappear by underreporting them or fudging their numbers or brazenly ignoring them altogether. We debated whether it would feel better to join a demo or duck Early Halloween entirely, in case plumping up the human density made a less than peaceful incident more likely, handing the media exactly the type of ugly image it televised and retelevised until you could see it with your eyes closed. Many assumed that was what the Republicans wanted—pictures of violent loony radicals wrestled to the ground by the heroic NYPD who had Professionalism, Courtesy, Respect, words to that effect, stenciled right on their patrol cars, and that's their thanks for selflessly risking life and limb in that horrible Towering Inferno all those folks in the Homeland watched on television.

Earlier that summer, two regular Friday political open-mike forums in Union Square had erupted into fistfights and bouts of shoving that somehow looked staged, the make-believe of paid provocateurs. But they could have been spontaneous assaults by fringe politicos bonkers from rage or deluded self-righteousness who spilled over the edge in unison. In which case, even if Karl Rove didn't plant activist impersonators to stir up shit, the left had its own assholes to do it for them.

It had been normal to feel paranoid since the election in 2000. Even more normal since 9/11.

In the cities I lived in, one on each coast, I never saw anybody pay the slightest mind to the color-coded alerts without laughing. You had to laugh, really, but it couldn't inspire much hilarity out in the Homeland, where people working three jobs to keep food on the family table had no time or mental energy for trying to think their way through a smoke screen of horseshit and really believed their chances of buying the farm in a WMD attack on Bohunk, Iowa, were "elevated" one day and "high" the next based on some factual evidence. Perhaps they were too rattled to notice the striking simultaneity of an especially alarming color and news of another administration claim exposed as a cynical fraud launched by some Pinocchio umbilically attached to George Bush.

Those of us who saw the towers come down in real time, from rooftops and balconies and apartment windows, weren't paranoid about gazillionaire terrorist Osama bin Laden and a bunch of cave-dwelling saps in Afghanistan. We figured that contingent had shot its wad, as far as Manhattan went. Las Vegas may advertise itself as the place where "what you do here stays here," but New York is the only such American city of nasty fun that will still have an aquifer layer in ten years. When the oil runs dry, these Al Qaeda people will have to go somewhere to get laid without the local imam finding out about it.

We pictured bin Laden anywhere but Tora Bora, sipping mai tais by the pool of the Manila Hilton while a twelve-year-old bar boy gave him a very spiritual blowjob. Islamic fanatics weren't nearly as scary as the fundamentalist Christians who were running the United States. Running it all the way to the Rapture, if the previous three years had been some really icky foreplay to put everybody in the mood.

In a videotape released to Al Jazeera shortly before the election, Osama bin Laden sounded like Voltaire compared to George W. Bush. At least 50 percent of what any psychopath says is true, whereas a petulant, congenitally embittered dry drunk can be a truly sadistic 24/7 liar.

The RNC landed on the city like Raymond Chandler's tarantula on a wedding cake. Originally, the Republicans picked New York for the ready-made photo op, another bonanza of valiant poses struck on the grave site of 3,000 people vaporized on 9/11. They imagined a replay of Bush with a megaphone rallying America behind him like Pavlov's famous dogs.

The chief-executive-at-the-site-of-tragedy scenario passed its expiration date once the city's blood pressure returned to something vaguely resembling normal, way before the RNC. Too many weird facts had leaked about 9/11, and presumably many more were in the pipeline. So far none of them had promoted any confidence that the president knew a fib from a fact, or meant what he said, or even knew what he meant.

Once it was too late to relocate the coronation to a region of easier marks, Oklahoma or Alabama, perhaps, the Grand Old Party, making lemonade from a lemon, recognized a deeply gratifying opportunity to flaunt contempt for a city whose rampant secularism and wholesale surrender to the "gay agenda" had prompted certain Republican evangelists to blame New York itself, its fags and abortionists, its satanic trends in "permissiveness," for the 9/11 terrorist attacks.

Even JC would have smitten the similar moral sewer of Sodom had He been around at the time. He had said, you know, that He came with a sword, a statement still vividly recalled by one of the Apostles, who wrote it down 200 years after He croaked. (Some insisted that He had said, "I cum with a sword up my ass," but this anathema went the way of the Albigensian heresy long before it could spread beyond the Cradle of Civilization, that Fertile Crescent so recently bombed into oblivion by the World's Only Superpower.) Even the Emperor Justinian, a limousine Christian if there ever was one, knew that sodomy caused earthquakes. Of course the theory of evolution and its minions had blinded people to the simple wisdom of ancient times, but tough titty for them, ancient times were here again.

It was soothing to this mind-set that New York City, aka Ground Zero, received anti-terrorist funding roughly equal to what rural Kansas got, but a special thrill to throw a huge, defiantly corny, triumphal fiesta in a city where people who richly deserved the suffering they'd already had would get a little more just knowing the RNC was whooping it up around the corner.

The heavy lifting required to translate the RNC overall theme, "A Safer World, A More Hopeful America," into a clear warning that a John Kerry victory virtually guaranteed another 9/11 fell to a quartet of differently moldy, vulpine patriots: Vice President Dick Cheney, a reliable flume of insatiable resentment; Senator Zell Miller, a rare kind of Democrat who smelled the traitorous stench rolling off John Kerry even before many twice-born Republicans had pointed their snouts in that direction; John McCain, who was either a great sport about those brainwashed-in-Hanoi phone calls down Carolina way or just creaming his boxers to get in front of a microphone—he was noted for that; and finally Rudy Giuliani, and what could you say about a man like Rudy Giuliani that he hadn't already said himself?

With the flair for grinning malice Rudy had perfected years earlier, when he paraded his cooze around in every upscale bistro in New York hoping to goad his wife-of-the-moment, Donna Hanover, into losing it right on her FoodTV show, the former Il Duce of the Big Apple told the enraptured delegates and press that "President Bush sees world terrorism for the evil that it is," whereas, he implied, John Kerry saw it for the evil it wasn't, that is, something that might easily diminish if the United States stopped sticking its six-guns into everybody else's business, like every Blame America First pantywaist.

John McCain echoed this conviction on behalf of the commander-in-chief whose every wish should be every American's ukase in times of war, such as these times of war, so menacing and dangerous a time that you practically had to flip a coin to decide which country to invade first. This war, indeed, was permanent, it would never end, somewhat like McCain's psoriasis, and every bit as flaky. He was the same bowel-impacted martinet he'd always been, even back when he couldn't help whining about his craving for candy bars to American antiwar visitors to Hanoi during his years in a "tiger cage." I've always wondered if those tiger cages weren't a bit more like pretty decent rooms at a Best Western, considering the gentle courtesy the Vietnamese are known for, even to people who wiped out several million of their countrypersons. I also can't imagine this xenophobia-stricken turd holding up to any sort of torture without singing like a canary, frankly, so I somehow doubt that his hardship in captivity required remotely the kind of stoicism everyone awards him such reflexive butt-licking credit for. God bless John McCain, heads throughout the hall sighed in smile language. If we threw him in a stew pot, he'd stand up and salt himself. That's the kind of patriotism America needs.

For sheer, unprincipled viciousness, however, nothing refreshed the gleaming twilight of the evening's heart-thumping spew like Zell Miller, a dropsical, mentally impaired Dixiecrat cut from the same chintz as Strom Thurmond. Who didn't adore chintz? Zell, or Zelig as he was sometimes called, drew the obvious parallel between World War II and the war in Iraq, the only difference between them being that World War II had ended practically all at once, and, naysayers such as John Kerry to the contrary, Iraq was an even more awesome success story, but the Iraqis themselves were proving too shiftless and lazy to root out this insurgency of foreign invaders. Anyone who said different was a turncoat, Zell could tell you, and did. John Kerry, half-Frog in the first place, "would let Paris decide when America needs defending." Moreover, Zell knew American values when he saw them. George Bush's "respect for his wife," "his unabashed love for his parents and his daughters," and his "unashamed belief that God is not indifferent to America" might not be useful experiences to list on your average minimum-wage job application, but the president's job had to answer to a higher power. If those who shit on God won the presidency, God would drop the biggest bowel movement in recorded history right back on the U.S. of A.

The "more hopeful America" RNC motif presented a tricky segue from the previous night of dark prognostication, for which Laura Bush was the ideal hope-meister, as she was known to care deeply about literacy and liked to remind people to leave no child behind, especially behind an SUV with its engine running. True, Laura had the charisma of a stale donut, but a stale donut dunked in a cup of yummy java tastes practically as fresh as a new one from Krispy Kreme. Anyway, you couldn't throw a convention without including some wistfully invented memories the candidate shared with the mother of his children.

Laura remembered that plain-jane Oldsmobile Cutlass they drove all over Texas the first time George ran for Congress. Sure, George's grandfather had made a pile with Averell Harriman fronting for that Nazi banker during WWII, and Senior was no slouch in the big grift department himself, but poor George had to ditch the Connecticut accent when he could barely speak English in the first place and learn how to waddle like a spavined ranch hand and paddle his way across a Lake Michigan of Jim Beam before he saw the Lord staring back at him from the ice cubes melting at the wrong end of a cocktail glass, on one of those rare nights when even he didn't dare to drive to the liquor store.

Laura remembered the laughs, the tears, the hardships. She remembered selling lids to her sophomore class at—no, she caught herself before the thought even reached the verbal cul-de-sacs in the canyons of her mind. Why should George be re-elected, some people asked her. The reasons were easy to fabricate. Health care. Prescription drug coverage for seniors. Stem cell research. George had cut off the funding for that so-called research in a principled way, "allowing science to explore its potential while respecting human dignity." Science's exploratory potential had exhausted the four superannuated stem cell lines they'd managed to isolate before that, but if wishes were horses, why, even beggars could ride. Home ownership at an all-time high. And of course, the threat of Manuel Noriega Khaddafi Kim Il Sung Saddam Hussein Fidel Castro Patrice Lumumba Salvador Allende or that other menace to our Free Society, I'm forgetting his name all of a sudden, oh yes, the Taliban, who had their good points, oil access and so forth, but really went too far, which George had finally squashed once and for all. And oh with what an ache of wonder and sweet gooey feeling Laura's nimble memory implants swept back to the endless skies and possibilities of West Texas, the optimism and promise of a simple, American place where dragging a Negro chained to a truck for several miles until he was scattered into several pieces was really the exception, not the rule.

The Bush Twins wowed the already wowed-to-the-max auditorium, adorable Valley Girls you just pictured at the Mall of America Tastee-Freez spooning their sundaes and giggling over that adorable guy who played Jed Clampett in the movie version of *The Beverly Hillbillies III*. Really, the Bushes had the same get-up-and-go, the same pizzazz, the same intimate knowledge of the American character as that family Faulkner wrote so much about—the Snopes, Snippers, something like that.

Other moments of powerful uplift included inspirational tunes by brave Gracie Rosenberger, who lost both legs in a car crash, which hadn't put her in a funk for one minute. And she hadn't puffed out all tubby like that comic Totie Fields did years ago after *her* legs got amputated.

Third Day, a group of "rockers" from Atlanta, sampled cuts from their latest album, which was top of the pops on the Nielsen SoundScan's Top Christian Albums chart.

Grammy-winning gospel vocalist Donnie McClurkin, whose "That's What I Believe" hit you right in the tear ducts, not only had a soul-stirring voice, as blacks so often do, but every inch of him inspired the Christian heart. His story just tore your strings. First of all some male relatives diddled him at age eight and again when he was thirteen. That had inflicted Homosexual Tendencies on him, immoral desires he'd agonized about for years, knowing it offended God even to think about allowing another's man's love to penetrate that place in every human soul designed for a woman's soul, however you wanted to put it. And contrary to the endless gay agenda propaganda that dominated the media hand in hand with treacherous anti-war liberals, Donnie had been cured of his obscene urges. One fine day, sickened by the prospect of the empty life of promiscuity these so-called gays got AIDS from, Donnie welcomed Jesus into his life, and Jesus singed off every last Inclination, the way a doctor will burn off a wart with a tiny electric medical implement.

Donnie hadn't taken the easy road, the greasy road, the road to cornholing and oral licking and sucking of sacred bodily areas and the other filthy things those people pretended they enjoyed so much. Letting a man's penis enter your rectum had to hurt; in fact, a number of wives on the convention floor could testify to that in court. No, Donnie didn't deserve that pain.

Donnie had reciprocated Jesus' favor by becoming senior pastor at Perfecting Faith in Freeport, New York. Only the other day, he announced an aggressive plan to battle "the curse of homosexuality," and you just knew he'd stay the course. Donnie wouldn't rest until every last fudge packer in the USA owned a pretty house in a tasteful suburb, with a sassy, adoring wife by his side and four little replicas cute as glove buttons.

All the same, Donnie *was* black. Even Jesus could only do so much. Anyway, why shouldn't he be black? It wasn't anything as bad as being gay. Donnie's RNC fans, thinking only of Donnie's happiness, did hope the cured new Donnie and others like him opted for suburbs where they would share a rich ethnic culture with their neighbors, instead of a predominantly white area where they were bound to feel Different, despite the generous welcome they'd get. Donnie had felt Different enough already for one courageous lifetime.

Perfected faith suffused the Republican National Convention like that extra Vicodin you weren't supposed to take but swallowed anyway to finish off a residue of toothache.

Americans of a certain vintage could recall an era when whole campaign speeches omitted any mention of religion. Entire presidential campaigns, in actual fact. There had been a time when a presidential candidate incapable of shutting up about his personal relationship with Jesus would have landed in a locked ward at Bellevue. That time was gone. Gone in the whirlwind.

Americans over forty discovered, here and there, on cable at 3 A.M. for example, kinescopes of speeches delivered by former presidents they could remember, like Dwight D. Eisenhower. Chancing on these figures instilled a kind of temporal vertigo. Memory jettisons so much of our lives as we move along: what to feel about it is as much a mystery as why we forgot an important thing and never got something minuscule out of our heads. The resurrection of forgotten voices, forgotten words, forgotten time, felt like blood rushing from the brain.

The political ectoplasms evoked the atmosphere of their time in a general way, and a trace of what life tasted like at a certain age, even if your personal minutiae stayed buried in Neverville. The nice part had to do with your survival through so much weirdness, and "emotion recalled in tranquillity"—the public people you despised when they were public people couldn't make you crazy any more, even grotesques like Bishop Fulton J. Sheen or John Foster Dulles. The disturbing part came as a recognition, at three in the morning, that the ghost of someone like Eisenhower now sounded as nuanced and rational and eloquent as Michelet.

When I forced myself to listen to a contemporary politician, I thought of a particular section in Burroughs's *Naked Lunch*. The one about "the man who taught his asshole how to speak."

Speaking of which: Bush's acceptance at the convention featured his signature blend of cosmetic self-portraiture, pandering in code, and an inventory of his "accomplishments"—initiatives and programs and innovations he claimed to have launched, for which he'd actually slashed all the funding. The economy was "growing again," the "frontiers of freedom" were expanding thanks to the American military "storming mountain strongholds and charging through sandstorms and liberating millions." If you imagined "the heart and soul of America is found in Hollywood," if you perceived some dangerous breach of the Constitution in "faith-based initiatives" and government support of religious institutions, if you trusted "activist judges" to protect the sanctity of marriage, you really ought to move to a depraved country like Canada. A devious repetition of the 9/11–Saddam Hussein link flickered past like a frame of subliminal advertising. "The soft bigotry of low expectations" tossed a tasty morsel of raw meat to rural communities in Mississippi where everyone was just family, in every sense of the word. Freedom was on the march—marching and freedom had become synonyms—and God would continue to bless America.

Bush could reel this doggerel off the teleprompter all night if he had to, a torrent of non sequiturs, in the zealous, whiny, pushy, straining voice of a man tormented by an image of Jack Daniels in the jumbo economy bottle flashing through his brain when he attempted two consecutive thoughts. He continued saying things after they were proven false. His favorite word was "belief." If you kept believing something, even something you'd made up yourself and knew wasn't true, other people might believe it, even force themselves to, avoiding the idea that a person compulsively repeating a delusional fantasy would probably be psychotic, or brainless.

The punctum of the RNC—the cum shot, so to speak—was neither the colorful ravings of Zell Miller, nor the infallibly hypnotic display of Rudy Giuliani's repugnant teeth. Nor was it the president's fulsome exhibition of clinical autism. It was Arnold Schwarzenegger.

A sea of awestruck delegates cheered themselves hoarse when The Terminator I and II, Mr. Total Recall and Kindergarten Cop himself, materialized at the podium. The ocean of Clairol-colored waves roiled and churned as though a volcano had spewed up a ton of magma from its darkest trench, gathering into a tsunami of rapturous faces and moist crotches and a visual blaze of straw boaters and flags and placards blazened with ARNOLD. It was the only RNC demonstration inside the Garden that seemed to release an authentic emotional unanimity, a fumigation of all doubt and hesitation from every inch of the convention hall. Next to Arnold, the president would have looked like a pansy. Arnold was lit up, Arnold's eyes blazed, Arnold smiled the way a man smiles when he's grabbed fate by the balls and run with it so many times he's never had to learn how to lose. It was a moment camera-ready for Leni Riefenstahl, and Arnold ran with that too.

Arnold Schwarzenegger's speech didn't register as the mindless, brutal affirmation of nationalist truisms that it was. His fanatical confidence, his zesty self-portrait as the American Dream's apotheosis, his proprietary manner of reciting every patriotic homily the audience had ever heard—the whole shebang had the sublimity of an epic fuck.

Arnold cast the mesmeric spell of his action pictures at those moments when the laws of physics and all cerebral interference disappeared in a blizzard of special effects, a Gotterdammerung fission blast of car chases and wrecked helicopters, scads of bleeding bodies flying everywhere, whole city blocks razed by whizzing debris.

True believers, for whom the majesty of purple mountains was no empty jingle, saw in the prehistoric warrior Arnold had played in so many films the dream politician for the Time of the Rapture: unafflicted by reflection, indifferent to scruple, and, unlike the obsequious ghouls who'd tit-tupped all over themselves on opening night, an old pro at instilling suspension of disbelief—all over the world, even with a stinkeroo like *Last Action Hero* dubbed into Arabic.

It was given that George Bush's pre-Sumerian syntax and shredded mental process made him like family to families deep in the Homeland's plaque-encrusted ventricles. The echo of their belief system—a suet of credulity, superstition, unhealthily excessive church attendance, and a gnashing, restive patriotism— yodeled back to them from the White House every day. Given too that the business end of the RNC prized Bush's knack for putting things over on people, found his pursy moues and sneers rather amusing, and reaped unimaginable cash rewards from his allergy to labor laws and pollution controls and anything else smacking of "special interests" of the weaker, humanistic kind. And then there were the dewy-eyed rubes in the cheapest seats, the ones who'd left Topeka for the first time ever to come here, righteous, clueless strivers who fell for aluminum siding scams and million-dollar magazine lotteries, the ones who had their heads so far up their asses the question of what was true and what wasn't was completely answered by who said it, since they couldn't hear anything up there anyway.

Yet it also was no secret that until his lucky day on September 11, 2001, George W. Bush had failed at virtually everything he'd ever done. He was failing now, failing in Iraq, failing in Afghanistan. The only thing he wasn't failing at was conning the marks and letting Karl Rove call the shots in the dirty tricks department, and if he really won this time he'd just go on failing at everything else. Winning or stealing an election didn't amount to shit anyway, compared with building a household appliance empire or starting a lucrative chain of specialty restaurants or, for that matter, becoming a rich and famous movie star. In that place and time, the Republicans, and G. W. Bush, needed Arnold Schwarzenegger a lot more than he needed them. Bush could yammer all he liked about the heart and soul of America not being in Hollywood. Fine. Who the fuck cared, save the heart and soul crap for people who'd never looked at Arnold's grosses and figured out what *was* in Hollywood—plenty more of it than you could squeeze from a bunch of trailer parks and Baptist churches. Truth be told, Arnold Schwarzenegger was everything George Bush wasn't. Including a "self-made man" in a number of sugar-sweet enterprises earning just fine, a record of actual business success.

If Arnold's American Dream was just as hallucinatory as Bush's, at least he had a palpable reason to believe in it, believe in it with the convert's fervor, the immigrant's passion, which always had more jizz than the rote convictions of somebody born and raised in pig heaven, money-wise, who graduated from Disneyland University thinking it was Yale.

When Arnold Schwarzenegger announced, on *The Tonight Show with Jay Leno,* his candidacy for governor of California in a special recall election that had been mandated by a statewide petition drive, the variegated solutions to the state's many problems proposed by other major candidates during the unusually compressed campaign period were not so much mooted as preempted, like a sporting event that preempts a regularly scheduled news broadcast.

It was as if the Queen of England had suddenly abdicated to stand for election in the House of Commons. Schwarzenegger's global celebrity belonged to a different order of magnitude than that of all but a few politicians. As a highly valued and valuable image in the world of images, Schwarzenegger conducted much of his campaign within that world, where the narcissism of other image-people complemented his. On *Leno, Oprah,* and other unchallenging entertainment programs where obsequiousness constitutes a job description, Arnold's appearances accomplished an almost subliminally imprinted conflation of the civic sphere and celebrity worship. The hosts and hostesses of these shows "meached" over this prized guest and were visibly exalted by his every grunt. Famous themselves, their function in the image world is the promotion of famousness as the apex of human endeavor. By his artful use of these venues, Schwarzenegger cultivated the impression that he was *condescending* to run for governor of California, an impression that carried an implication of *sacrifice,* which in turn could only be accounted for by a powerful wish to serve the public.

On television, at shopping mall rallies, in civic auditoriums, and wherever else Arnold's majesty happened to present itself, the long-incubated woes besetting California became a collection of keywords—*taxes, illegal immigrants, Sacramento,* and a shortlist of others. For "programs," Schwarzenegger's best-known bits of movie dialogue substituted as blocky "messages": The people wanted *action, action, action*. For Gray Davis, the current governor whose removal from or retention in office was the first decision voters had to make on the recall ballot, it was going to be *hasta la vista, baby*. The eternal gridlock in the Sacramento legislature, *no problemo*. The budget deficit, the energy crisis, the imminent hike in car registration fees, the high taxes driving businesses out of California would all be *terminated* by Conan the Barbarian himself.

This language of coercion, plucked from fictions that glorified force as the preferred method of problem-solving, formed an intoxicating, vaporous mirage in the sketchy shape of a political "platform." The Schwarzenegger bandwagon was a flying carpet, floating elusively between the hemorrhoid-crimson Mars of *Total Recall* and the carnage-strewn freeways of *Terminator 2*, films in which the candidate rescued humanity from slavery and annihilation.

"Sending a message," in recent times, has become a ubiquitous phrase in America's political vocabulary, one that reflects a mental fusion of action and language, and at the same time a complete separation of language from meaning. Doing something is, first and foremost, saying something. This notion has gained a certain purchase on the public imagination, and has the effect of dematerializing physical reality, transforming aggressive actions and punitive alterations of the social contract into abstract singing telegrams.

Invading a country, for example, is only incidentally an invasion. It is, first and foremost, a "message" to certain people, many people, most people, or all people, a "message" to disobedient countries, a "message" to that inchoate formation of "evildoers"

George Bush so often mentions, a "message" its intended recipients ignore at their peril. Massive tax cuts "send a message" to the virulent and implacable proponents of "big government," while their actual effect of further enriching the wealthy and further impoverishing the poor is an inconsequent by-product of the message.

A message can take all sorts of forms. Voting for Arnold Schwarzenegger "sent a message" of brand loyalty to a consumer product, a public image, an icon of power.

"We have businesses leaving here every day. We have people leaving the state every day. We see a budget that is the biggest budget deficit that we've ever had in the history of California. We see our ratings, the junk bond ratings that we're getting, it is disastrous. We see a governor being recalled. We see an education system that is the last in the country. We just see things declining and declining and declining. And the biggest problem that we have is, that California has been run now by special interests. All of the politicians are not anymore making the moves for the people, but for special interests and we have to stop that.

"So this is why I'm running for governor. I will go to Sacramento and I will clean house. I will change that. As you know, I don't need to take any money from anybody. I have plenty of money myself. I will make the decisions for the people" (Arnold Schwarzenegger, August 6, 2003, following his appearance on *The Tonight Show with Jay Leno*).

TWO

"Personal branding" and "marketed authenticity" factored into the California recall election with innovative virulence. The election served as a springboard for various "personalities" to make themselves known, or better known, or known in a different sense than previously.

Within the lucrative realm of prescriptive self-help books, seminars, encounter groups, and sects, a growing industry inspired by the encroachment of the image world into the sphere of unmediated reality markets techniques for transforming the individual into a "personal brand"—not a person, necessarily, but a collage of quirks, consumer preferences, sexual wishes, hobbies, and opinions. One captain of this industry defines a personal brand as "a perception or emotion, maintained by somebody other than you, that describes the total experience of having a relationship with you."

The demand for this particular pseudoscience gives an entirely new meaning to the term "self-storage." To become an image, a holographic projection of one's idealized self, presenting to the world something both more and less than a human being: this project is qualitatively different than a public image acquired as the result of extraordinary accomplishment, or, for that matter, exceptional villainy. Fame as a goal in and of itself is the will to power at its most atavistic extreme.

In "serious," mainstream reporting, the carnivalesque travesty spawned by the California recall was generally handled as a sideshow act, while the possible removal of the state's highest elected official, and the question of who, if he were removed, might be elected to replace him, occupied the center ring.

Yet the scramble of hundreds of Californians to get their names on the ballot, and the remarkable number and variety who did, demonstrated that popularity, in no discernible political sense, and personal recognition, in the most exhibitionistic sense, could become the foremost "issues" decided by the eventual vote. And they did. Schwarzenegger's entry enhanced the recall's resemblance to a race for the presidency of a high school class. He spearheaded the geek division of the gubernatorial race, becoming its only well-known-enough representative. Like the infinitely lesser known geeks, Arnold ran for governor because he could run for governor.

True, he had plans. Plans for the state, plans for the problems, plans for all the menu items every politician has plans for. Schwarzenegger had plenty of plans for Schwarzenegger—he'd always had plans for Numero Uno, and all these other plans were instrumental. As Kant more eloquently wrote in "Fundamental Principles of the Metaphysics of Morals," *"I ought to do something, on this account, because I wish for something else."* Or, to reverse a famous platitude of John F. Kennedy, ask not what you can do for your country, but what your country can do for you.

Arnold was as familiar as any canned tuna or packaged cake the average voter might pick up at Ralph's. A brand name like StarKist or Entenmann's. His weirdly overdeveloped physique, like Barbra Streisand's nose or Dolly Parton's tits, first appeared in the public realm as a risible novelty. It's the nature of American grotesquerie, however, to persist in a space where it doesn't fit, for decades if necessary, wearing down all resistance. The grotesque then reconfigures the space in its own image.

Arnold's bizarre physicality advanced in stages from fringe to center, from sight gag to fetish to archetype, from a specialized, coterie taste to an international trademark. Millions had a perception or emotion of "having a relationship" with him. This constituency of ticket buyers was spread throughout California, even in odd pockets like Eureka and Independence.

The August 2004 issue of *ArtUS,* a Los Angeles–based magazine, features an essay by the artist Richard Hawkins describing, among other things, a hilarious inventory of Arnoldiana he's collected over the years, including editions of Plato's *Symposium* and Arthur Symons's *Love's Cruelty* the star inscribed and autographed for him when Hawkins worked in a used book store.

Other Hawkins treasures include a physique magazine from 1966, *MANual,* containing "two photos of a bikini-clad teenage Arnold," who, according to the caption, "works in a feather-plucking factory and specializes in dyeing bird plumage." More items: nude photos of Arnold from "the February 1977 *After Dark* and the April 1986 *Playgirl*"; "ten miscellaneous tear sheets documenting Schwarzenegger's association with Joe Weider . . . responsible for importing Arnold from Austria to California in

1969, fronting him a salary of $100 a week for King Kong–style 'publicity stunts' and 'feats of strength.' " Schwarzenegger's role (as evinced by his inclusion in muscle mags of the '60s, as well as gay-themed publications of the '70s) in the cross-germinative progression of body-built male imaging and gay representation from the '60s onward (which, by the way, carries with it what I have referred to in another text as the "breastification" of physi-ological hyper-masculinity) and its connection, in taking another turn, to the politics of assimilation, which almost always are char-acterized by a curve from outside to center and from marginal to conservative (Richard Hawkins, "Devil May Sign," 2004).

The shape-shifting Hawkins describes is what we might de-fine as the Epitome of Arnold. Schwarzenegger's "personal brand" is a compilation of re-inventions, an advertisement for itself, a personality remarkable for its periodic shedding of layers. A compost heap that smells, at first, good to the few who savor the smell of compost, eventually to many who acquire the predilection in imitation of the few, ultimately to a consensus large enough to rechristen the compost heap as a rose garden. This may illustrate a systemic flaw in the concept of democracy, especially but not exclusively "direct democracy" of the type envisioned by the reformers of the California constitution, who instituted a recall statute so easily deployed that it can just as readily serve demagoguery and *ressentiment* as "democracy."

Outside to center, marginal to conservative, station to station: the breastified Arnold enjoyed a long run, and this image served its purpose during a period when the leather look, the Tom of Finland gigantism, stopped only a few perceptual centimeters short of the Botero painting look few people acquire deliberately, and temporarily defined the Image of Perfection in "gay culture." Not for all gay men, perhaps not even for many gay men, in actual fact. But "gay culture," from the time of the Stonewall Riots to the assimilationist "mainstreaming" of homosexuality, passed through a series of fetishistic and exclusionary idealizations of what an "attractive" homosexual looked like. When Arnold was still pumping iron for a living, his gym-inflated body was the flavor of the day.

Knowing whether or not Arnold had homosexual affairs, or tricks, or made himself available for close encounters of the tearoom kind wouldn't alter the image of Arnold in any significant way at this moment, at least, though if it were known for a fact that he did have them, it might very well impede his political ambitions in the future. What the "material" behind an image does in the material world has flexible relevance, determined by the nature of the image. Real actions detrimentally affect an image only if the image projects the idea that its proprietor would not, could not, or should not do this, that, or the other.

Arnold's "gay friendly" attitude throughout his career has worked to his advantage in the accumulation of fame. If we think of him as a free-range ego on a mission to build the largest possible following, making his image "available" in an unambiguously gay consumer market in the sixties and seventies should be read as consensus-building. The consistent assertion of his basic heterosexual identity makes the "gay friendly" identification easily reversible, in rhetorically well-crafted increments, should it develop into a liability in the years ahead. The key to self-marketing, as per its swamis, is creating "a perception or emotion of having a relationship" with the product. The goal, creating that perception or emotion in as many people as possible.

• • •

Consider *Terminator* and *Terminator 2* as a two-volume meta-phorized, primal autobiography: in the first film, Arnold plays a machine sent to the past from the future to eliminate Sarah Connor, who will give birth to the future destroyer of the machine's manufacturers, who are themselves machines. Simultaneously, a human male "resistance fighter," by the same inexplicable time-traveling process, materializes to guard a cosmically significant pregnancy from termination, or, bluntly stated, to prevent an abortion. Implacably, the Terminator hunts down his prey by killing several Sarah Connors listed in the phone book, and many other people, too. Yet the human time-traveler thwarts the Terminator's mission, albeit at the expense of his own life. The Terminator is killed, or, more accurately, disassembled, crushed, and pulverized by Sarah Connor herself.

In *Terminator 2,* John Connor, son of Sarah, is a boy of twelve or thirteen. His mother has languished in a mental hospital for an unspecified number of years. Her apparently compulsive warnings of the impending nuclear war that caused the future the first Terminator came from to exist have been diagnosed as delusional schizophrenia.

Meanwhile, a more advanced model of Terminator has been flushed down the ever-unelucidated memory hole to eliminate John Connor. The human "resistance" the future John Connor will lead, somehow (as in the original film) fully informed of the precise details of the android race's machinations, beams down the original Terminator, Arnold, reprogrammed to protect the boy from the new Terminator. Since this ur-Terminator was irreversibly terminated before, how it's been reconstituted—by its master's enemies, no less—may be a conundrum of time travel only the future could explain. Alternatively, why "the resistance" would create and time-transport an identical twin of the evil Terminator with reversed imperatives in its hard drive can only imply that the ideal human simulacrum has the form of Arnold Schwarzenegger, the classic model superseded by a less humanly powerful-looking one made of liquid metal that's capable of re-shaping itself into copies of human beings, of merging with inanimate materials, and, if shattered into many pieces, automatically recombinant.

Despite the chasms of disbelief viewers have to suspend themselves across, the first two Terminator films are the best action films Schwarzenegger ever made, and incidentally contain the first hints of his inherent gift (I'd hesitate to call it flair) for comedy. They operate on paradox and metamorphoses, a witty creepiness and inventive violence, visual ingenuity and a fairly high quality of acting.

Arnold is the killing machine of the first film and the protective, humanitarian machine of the second. The two are physically identical, oppositely programmed servomechanisms. On the rare occasions they speak, they do so with the same voice. They possess the same superhuman strength and other special powers superior to those of humans.

Schwarzenegger's films are often variations on the theme of an unchanging figure whose interiority is completely reversible. At the same time, these characters have no discernible interiority more complex than the rudimentary moral reflex that motivates their violent behavior for either "good" or "evil." In some sense, Schwarzenegger's performances offer an inverted literalization of the hypothesis often entertained about actors and acting—that an actor assumes a succession of artificial identities because there is no legible "self" behind the persona. Arnold's persona remains fixed, while the "self" he dramatizes can be discarded and replaced with an entirely different one, like a mask.

If I've managed to suggest that Schwarzenegger lacks complexity, that isn't uniformly true and possibly the least true thing one could say about him. It would be more accurate to say that Schwarzenegger's complexity manifests itself in peculiar ways, among them the recasting of clichés as epic myths and unpredictable strategies of self-simplification.

The Terminator twins reenact the primal situation. The first Terminator issues from an evil and intrinsically regimented race of automata, a patriarchal order intent on eliminating a race of soft-bodied, presumably "democratic" enemies possessing non-utilitarian emotional components. This paternity evokes the figure of Schwarzenegger's father, a Nazi Party member who was the police commissioner of Graz, Austria. The Terminator's physicality and single-minded pursuit of a threat to the father mirror the senior Schwarzenegger's reportedly iron discipline and harsh authoritarian personality.

The second Terminator issues from an implied matriarchy, since the original threat to the father was not John Connor but the woman who would give birth to him. While Terminator 2 arrives after John Connor's birth, and isn't programmed to rescue his mother, his programmed obedience to the son makes the mother's liberation from the asylum and escape from the "other" Terminator the film's fulcrum.

The "soft" human qualities of the mother, combined with the "hard," goal-oriented nature of the father, produce the ideality of Schwarzenegger–Terminator. He is the exemplar of a Master Race, the humans of the future toughened by military discipline while retaining "emotions." As recombined by the future human race his existence is designed to create, T2 is "deeply hostile towards his strict, authoritarian father and strongly attached to his indulgent, hard-working mother," as Robert Wistrich's *Who's Who in Nazi Germany* describes Adolf Hitler.

Every master race needs its Fuhrer and its myth of origin: while far less cinematically satisfying, *Terminator 3: The Rise of the Machines* is an appropriate pendant to the diptych, as the nuclear holocaust the human time traveler and the reprogrammed Schwarzenegger of *T2,* respectively, warned about is finally at hand. The android in Schwarzenegger form reappears, years after *T2* wraps up, not only to ensure the survival of the young adult John Connor, who's become a nihilistic pill freak and loser, but also that of a young veterinarian, Kate Brewster, who might have been his high school sweetheart if John hadn't been such a fuck-up at the time.

After an amazingly bizarre series of escapes from a back-from-the-future, even more souped-up Terminatrix (TX, as she's called)—suggestive, among other things, of how much pleasure the writers and producers of this film get from imagining endlessly novel ways of mutilating a female body—which lead to a peculiarly half-assed, failed effort to prevent Armageddon, Schwarzenegger/android, knowing all along the end couldn't be prevented (although, if everything's inevitable, how sending him back in time to change the future really helps matters, you tell me), spirits Kate and John to a nuke-proof bunker somewhere in one of the red states, where, alone together in this womblike facility, they become the sole survivors of the catastrophe outside, presumably to spawn an all-new human race, Adam and Eve to the Terminator's God.

This film destroys the artful symmetry of its two prequels, but completes this series with a logical and unsettling conclusion: the robotic blend of disciplinarian father and warm but militarized mom isn't simply there to rescue the Aryan progenitors of a harsh, unwelcomingly flattened planet's future humans; he is himself Nietzsche's Superman, as human as anyone needs to be, and, in every sense, better than human, the Creator of humanity as well as its Savior. If there is ever a *T4*, Schwarzenegger would presumably materialize from the future of the future in the form of a winged creature, as the Holy Ghost of the three-in-one Catholic deity, perhaps to prevent Kate from chomping any fruit off the Tree of Knowledge. His opponent, of course, would be an implacably prehensile female anaconda.

One has to preempt the argument that Arnold Schwarzenegger didn't write or direct the films he appeared in, from *The Terminator* forward, by stipulating that he had originally been offered the more expository and ostensibly heroic role of Reese, the "human throwback" played by Michael Biehn, and himself opted for the film's barely verbal, robot villain, a part in which James Cameron had envisioned Jurgen Prochnow. Sean French, in *The Terminator,* a masterful analysis of the film (BFI Modern Classics, BFI Publishing, 1996, pp. 30–31), quotes Cameron as saying, "With Arnold, the film took on a larger-than-life sheen. I just found myself on the set doing things I didn't think I would do— scenes that were supposed to be purely horrific that just couldn't be, because now they were too flamboyant."

To quote French himself: "This alteration was not due to any insight brought to the role by Schwarzenegger himself. Shrewd as he is, Schwarzenegger's analysis of his own work has generally been restricted to its importance for his long-term strategy in the industry."

The Terminator made Arnold a big enough box office draw that he could pick and choose his projects, injecting his wishes into scripts and deciding what things he would say—generally, as little as possible. And, of course, scripts written specifically with Schwarzenegger in mind became bankable if Schwarzenegger chose to sign on for them.

It's been speculated in more than one magazine profile that Maria Shriver, Schwarzenegger's politically sophisticated spouse, strongly influenced the actor's surprisingly successful forays into comedies. It's also been suggested that Shriver wrote most of Schwarzenegger's speech for the RNC.

It is completely evident to anyone who's watched Schwarzenegger's entire filmic oeuvre (a less punishing experience than one would imagine) that from *The Terminator* through Schwarzenegger's last movie, *T3,* only the least lucrative efforts failed to reflect the same narrow set of themes, the same "messages," the same conflations of virtue with the cleverly triumphant deployment of physical strength and "strong leadership" in service to "the right idea."

All but a handful of these many movies qualify in one sense or another as science fiction, the perfect genre for making the same message original-looking on the most superficial yet most hypnotic level.

"The past meant nothing to Arnold because it was over," the director of *Pumping Iron,* George Butler, told the *New York Times* in August 2003. "He never looked over his shoulder. This is a man of bottomless ambition. It's always been there. He sees himself as almost mystically sent to America."

Pumping Iron was not Schwarzenegger's first film, nor even the first good film he appeared in: the risibly awful *Hercules in New York* was his first "starring" role, though Arnold's presence in it was more akin to the "King Kong–like feats of strength" for which the oleaginous muscle impresario Joe Weider had previously paid him $100 a pop. Arnold was a bit player in Robert Altman's first-rate film *The Long Goodbye,* barely registering as scenery, for less than a minute of screen time.

But before *Pumping Iron,* which made Arnold famous *as* Arnold Schwarzenegger—bodybuilder, good-natured freak, and presumed simpleton—far beyond the brackets of the audience of enthusiasts of that particular "sport," Arnold carried an impressive major role in Bob Rafelson's *Stay Hungry,* as third lead to Jeff Bridges and Sally Field, that exploited his bodybuilding prowess to the max, but also displayed his ability to project a personality considerably more nuanced than, and even at times surprisingly unlike, the stereotype of slow-witted eminence in a submental marginal sport his body itself suggested.

Both *Pumping Iron* and *Stay Hungry* are significantly well-wrought films, one fiction, the other a documentary. *Stay Hungry* is perhaps the only film in which Schwarzenegger has acted really effectively: that is, his character exhibits a remarkable worldliness while appearing entirely guileless, a sweet child trapped in a ridiculously pneumatic adult body—not an innocent child, but one who's developed an almost Zen acceptance of things. In *Pumping Iron* the manchild reveals his propensity for bullying, for psyching out his best friend, another competitor—he fights dirty, so to speak, with a smiling incomprehension of any value other than winning. While the "real" Schwarzenegger of *Pumping Iron* is more or less the same Schwarzenegger in *Stay Hungry,* Bob Rafelson, as director of the latter film, has supplied him with a certain ethical restraint in screenplay form.

George Butler's mystical view of Arnold's inexhaustible ambition recommended itself to the moment's general mood when the California recall election caromed quickly from gross unlikelihood to fait accompli. The past meant nothing to voters, either. Not the pre–Davis administration past of Pete Wilson's governorship, which had brought disaster to California by privatizing its public utilities and selling them off to Texas energy companies, key members of whose elite Schwarzenegger depended upon for advice. Efforts to mine Schwarzenegger's personal history for the kind of scandal that sometimes derails political ambitions (the resignation of Governor James McGreevey of New Jersey a year later comes to mind—a veritable snakepit of weirdness, in which a married politician came out of the closet, at least partly to obscure the rich and entirely unrelated corruption his administration engaged in) caused a virulent blowback against journalists and newspapers, particularly against the *Los Angeles Times,* which had published the results of a three-month investigation of Schwarzenegger's past behavior.

The unresonant reception of the *Times* series was later blamed on its bad timing, the compressed campaign period, and vigilant damage control. But the actual failure of charges and allegations to revise the "exceptionalism" of Schwarzenegger's established image, which was qualitatively different than a politician's, had as much to do with the public's indifference to reality as it had to its related worship of manufactured symbols.

• • •

A short digression on the condition of the public sphere in which Arnold Schwarzenegger was elected governor of California: we should consider today's culture of corrupted journalism, and its complicity with Arnold's almost effortless neutralization of reported, highly credible allegations, by at least nine women, that surfaced in the *Los Angeles Times* after a long investigation, that the actor had unwelcomingly and humiliatingly groped and fondled these women in separate incidents throughout his Hollywood career. This was hardly all. Many previous accusations had been made about Schwarzenegger's obnoxious sexual behavior, one from a black bodybuilding opponent whose wife (who confirmed his story) Schwarzenegger allegedly seduced. Postcoitally, Schwarzenegger dialed a number from the bedside telephone, then handed the receiver to the woman, who was horrified to discover the voice on the other end was her husband's. Schwarzenegger grabbed the phone and barked into it, "*I just fucked her. I just fucked your wife.*"

It's true that these and similar allegations never quite seemed enough for a criminal indictment. When a person wishes to control important aspects of many other people's lives, however, with the force of law behind him, outright criminal behavior in someone's past, depending on the nature of it, can be less revealing than the technically legal abuse of power that someone who has it has already exercised, albeit power in a slightly different realm. (As Arnold's own shill Jay Leno once accurately put it, "Politics is show business for ugly people.")

It's also true that Schwarzenegger never actually denied any of the accusations, but gave the ponderous excuse that he'd done certain things that he now understood were wrong, thinking at the time they were funny. Well, so have we all. But molesting women isn't something an adult man in Austria does with the intention of being funny, so the implied excuse that his cultural background made Schwarzenegger understandably behave like an especially ill-bred ten-year-old—for instance, sticking his hand up a woman's blouse and squeezing her breast without her consent—could only have any plausibility to a population that regarded the world beyond its own borders as entirely alien and unknowable. Just as the history of political mistakes in its own culture seemed beyond the reach of consciousness for an alarming segment of Americans—at the very least, a 1 percent majority of the 50 percent of eligible voters who participated in the 2004 presidential election—a basic inability to distinguish right from wrong seemed positively endearing to them when exhibited by an immigrant who had staunchly embraced America as his chosen home without fully understanding all its uniquely civilized ways. They even found it charming in the homegrown, flag-waving wastebasket they voted in as President.

The "issue" that developed around this series of stories—one that could only seem relevant in an ostensibly free society driven by fantasy and denial rather than common sense—reflects the ever-raised ante of the bait-and-switch technique modern journalism and its consumers have fallen prey to. It indicates, too, the self-cannibalizing nadir to which the practice of reporting in the United States has degenerated.

It is, in fact, the inevitable dead end modern journalism was fated to meet from its inception, a moment that Alexander Cockburn brilliantly located and analyzed in a 1975 essay, "The Psychopathology of Journalism," in the *New York Review of Books*. Cockburn identified the turning point where journalism became something other than—or, strictly speaking, merely—objective reporting, insofar as a lack of personal bias is possible. Not simply the reporting of facts that are not news at all in a sensational sense, but facts of manifest public benefit to know, or of important news that every newspaper (and now, television and radio) would cover, but a mind-altering bombardment of indeterminably true and false and in-between effusions of contradictory assertions based on anything at all, or nothing at all, whose purveyors' highest value is "breaking news" *before* anyone else. This eventually redefines news as entertainment with no intrinsic relation to truth, or as actual events of no importance to the general population inflated into earthshaking significance, like a banal murder or the trial of its perpetrator, or even things that aren't events, like the "projections" of television networks during an election, disseminated *before* anyone else. The factual content of a "story" has practically nothing to do with the urgency with which its sensational potential is exploited, whatever its truth content turns out to be—by the time the more lingering trivial or even important questions are answered, the questions themselves have become "old news," the truth of the matter at hand being of no interest whatever compared with the thrill of its mindless novelty.

This has everything to do with how an individual like Arnold Schwarzenegger—whose lack of interest in anyone's well-being besides his own, and that of his enablers, so to speak, is so blatantly inscribed on his entire career, and who was hardly shy about saying so himself until he decided to become "a public servant"—gets to "play" being the chief executive of the world's sixth largest economy. Not to digress from my digression:

Ultimately, we arrive at the "event" of the reporting of news *as* the news, replacing hard reality with a culture of ideologically twisted imperviousness to facts. Such was the fate of the *Los Angeles Times* series on Schwarzenegger's history of otiose behavior.

The series would not have been publishable by a major newspaper if it weren't verifiable to the satisfaction of many extremely prudent attorneys. Instead of being praised for casting a justifiably bright light on the character flaws of someone seeking power over the daily lives of Californians, the *Times* was widely vilified by America's recent breed of television anchorpersons, who are, by and large, simply actors employed by television franchises, paid to fill lavishly underwritten advertising time with whatever nonsense passes through their minds. This species, which has more or less colonized the widest audience of American media consumers, stigmatized the L.A. *Times* for "playing politics," simply because it printed what its reporters—real ones, or as close to real ones as we have any more—had managed to learn in three months. The "timing" of the story became the story.

It's some measure of the gulf between current public perception and reality that the word "politics" is widely taken to mean, *io ipso,* something negative, a dirty trick, something beneath contempt, while those who exercise real power in America are above anything as tawdry as "playing politics." The distribution of power is also, obviously, assumed to be something conferred by regal privilege, over which the assertion of the citizen's right to know as much about who gets it as possible, and to cast a vote with any greater knowledge of the person asking for it than "a perception or feeling" of "having a relationship" with his image, is beyond the pale of acceptability. This seems the rather terrifying but logical result of widespread imbecilization by power-hungry demagogues who have, since Ronald Reagan—a shill for

General Electric and 20 Mule Team Borax prior to becoming governor of California himself—demonized "big government," and finally just "government," while seizing control of it, and denounced "playing politics" as anything interfering with their demolition of American democracy.

Henri Georges Stephan Adolphe de Blowitz (1825–1903) became a journalist in France during Napoleon III's Second Empire. An incredibly well-connected, classically educated, monied aristocrat, de Blowitz was the first reporter to employ the "inside source" as a method of scooping others who would report the same thing slightly later than he did. As the Franco-Prussian War neared its end, the London *Times* hired de Blowitz as its European correspondent to cover the Congress of Berlin, ostensibly convened to calm the general residue of the 1877–1878 Russo-Turkish War. The dominant figures were Prime Minister Disraeli of Great Britain and Chancellor Otto von Bismarck of Germany. Bismarck wanted the proceedings of the Congress kept entirely secret, and went to elaborate lengths to have his intelligence service prevent any leakage, even if it entailed arresting and detaining people; de Blowitz's immense network of socially powerful friends enabled him to get his own Deep Throat (de Blowitz's was not fictitious, as Woodward and Bernstein's was) appointed as an attaché to the Congress. Via this contact, he achieved a series of scoops that appeared, unsigned, in the London *Times*.

The story of how de Blowitz and his planted informant communicated is fascinating in itself, but de Blowitz has a place in the history of journalism solely because he published, on June 22, 1878, the terms of the Treaty of Berlin virtually as it was being signed, and many hours before its release to the world press.

As Cockburn cites from de Blowitz's memoirs, "To have published an important document before anybody else does not make you a great writer or even a great journalist." Cockburn adds: "Evidently de Blowitz could see that detached readers might well have asked what exactly was the point of a feat in which the *Times* of London managed to print a document on a Saturday only through prodigious efforts and enormous expense, whereas this same document was freely distributed to every journalist in Berlin shortly afterward."

De Blowitz's accomplishment was, in fact, the transformation of a fact's importance from its basic content to the *speed* at which it became public—an emphasis that has become so defining of contemporary reporting that getting at the truth of things has taken a tertiary or even a nonexistent role in daily journalism.

The swift dissemination of unverified rumors, gossip that becomes far more deeply embedded in the public's mind than any subsequent retraction of it, has at last come full circle: the results of a scrupulous investigation into credible charges against a person running for public office become a matter of public debate—not over what the investigation revealed, or failed to prove, but over *why the results were reported when they were*—that is, before the person under investigation had won election to a powerful public position.

This phenomenon bears a curious resemblance to the "reasoning" behind the U.S. Supreme Court's decision in favor of George W. Bush in *Bush v. Gore* after the presidential election of 2000: a carefully monitored, meticulous recount of the ballots citizens cast in an extraordinarily close state election—a matter of fewer than 200 votes—was declared impermissible because it would "cast a cloud" over George Bush's *claim* that he had won the election. As Renata Adler's dissection of *Bush v. Gore* (*Irreparable Harm,* Melville House Books, 2004) elucidates, this was, in effect, the Court ruling against the defendant on the grounds that the plaintiff's *claim* that he had been elected might be "clouded"—or even disproven!—by a recount.

This had much to do with the regressive, one-justice majority on the U.S. Supreme Court and its flagrant partisanship, of course, but the election itself had been thrown into question, initially, by the premature "awarding" of Florida by one television network to Al Gore, and the subsequent intervention in what was, in fact, a prediction rather than a fact, by a Bush relative with powerful media connections, reversing the "projection" of Gore's victory before all the ballots were counted—before, in fact, many actual ballots had been counted at all. The projection of who won became more decisive than a factual determination of who won.

De Blowitz didn't invent the practice of making important things into trivia and trivial things into gigantic public concerns. This has always been a favorite stratagem of totalitarian dictators and avaricious tribes, has launched countless wars, and is the specialty of George W. Bush's brain, as Karl Rove is so often aptly called. De Blowitz himself was astonished at how his reporting coup became something more than a clever scoop. As he went to considerable trouble and ingenuity to get it, we can't really say that he's the father of modern journalism, either.

It is no more important today than it was in 1878 to know the exact wording of a peace treaty that's already been signed a day before it is publicly released, compared to the fact that peace has been declared. In fact, the parsing of such a document in advance of its disclosure tends to inflate the very antagonisms that caused a war in the first place. (Paradoxically, the most important documents that Americans should see in such a timely manner are sealed for as long as fifty to one hundred years by the government, at which time the outrage they might have mobilized has been entirely dissipated by the passage of time. George W. Bush has taken this secrecy—more like a mafioso protection racket than anything resembling statecraft—further than any president in American history, by classifying his own official documents, and his father's, and those of all future presidents beyond anyone's natural lifespan.)

Yet little innovations like de Blowitz's have a way of reverberating to catastrophic effect. The "inside source" has become the "anonymous source" of legend. The anonymity of journalists' sources was initially protected by law to shield powerless people against retribution from powerful people. As Renata Adler has written in several excoriating essays on the contemporary press, today the "anonymous source" is almost always a powerful person, and can usually be identified by discerning which person named in a news story is treated most generously.

Another disastrous development in modern journalism, which Adler noted several decades ago in her first novel, *Speedboat,* is recent enough to account for my lifelong inability to remember the name of a reporter after reading a news article in the *New York Times* or any other American newspaper: in a less artificial and celebrity-driven time, newspaper reporting was almost invariably anonymous.

I grew up assuming that a newspaper, whatever its obvious or subtly inflected bias, purveyed it with as little assertion of its reporters' own identities as humanly possible. News was not the inscription of an individual on historical events, or even on a traffic accident. Opinion columnists, reviewers, and the like, of course, have always had a by-line, but reporters of fact were considered the institutional voice of the paper publishing their reports. When news reporters on television began becoming highly paid celebrities, this practice disappeared: the reporters themselves wanted to be "news."

The resulting perversities of celebrity journalism have manifested themselves in innumerable ways. An opinion columnist like Bob Novak, for example, becomes a "news reporter" when he publishes the name of a CIA operative as an operative himself for the U.S. government's executive branch as retribution against one of its own employees, the CIA operative's spouse. And because he has breached the former firewall between opinion writing and news reporting, he becomes "immune" from "revealing his anonymous source," that is, the government itself, and enjoys the institutional protection of the news reporting functions of the institution that prints his opinion column. Novak is, after all, just another newspaper writer who, like the paper's actual reporters, happens to have a by-line.

The *Los Angeles Times* series on Schwarzenegger, on the other hand, was researched by a large team of authentic reporters, whose actual names were only given to indicate how many reporters had worked on it. When challenged about the anonymity of certain of its informants, the informants themselves came forward and identified themselves. The series had utter transparency in terms of who reported it and who their sources were, and the paper freely admitted that it published the series a few days before rather than immediately after the recall election because it—institutionally "it"—considered it in the public interest to know the story before rather than after voters chose what candidate should run the state of California. The paper was accused of having "sat on the report" long after it was filed in order to release it at a "strategic" moment that proved so obviously "politically motivated" that the strategy backfired. In reality, the paper had only fully checked and rechecked the verifiable facts of a series of reports that its reporters had just finished filing.

So there was only one "timing" issue: whether to print a series of news reports that had just become publishable a week before the election, or some time after the election. The paper's editors considered it a matter of civic interest to publish the story before the election. It would, after all, have no legitimate civic function if published afterwards, and their decision was, obviously, a "political" one, a quite legitimate political decision. But such decisions, like anything else that asserts the public interest within the public sphere, instantly fall victim to the demonization of "politics" as an unfair and scurrilous "game" undermining the prerogatives of people seeking, or possessing, power.

The breathtaking hypocrisy of those determined to see a Hollywood star of their own political inclinations willing to dismiss his "youthful indiscretions," none of which had occurred during his youth, but as recently as three years previously, as "accepted Hollywood behavior" that occurred on what Schwarzenegger characterized as "rowdy movie sets" (a fabulously weird adjective to apply to any contemporary movie set, especially the sets of movies in which hundreds of millions of dollars are invested, as studio chief Sherry Lansing was quick to explain to reporters)— the very voters, that is, whose demonization of Hollywood as the epitome of "immorality" aggressively destroying the country's "moral values"—demonstrates the implacable determination of the Republican agenda as exemplified by the *Bush v. Gore* decision. Part of this agenda is to remake the cultural sphere in the image of its "values." The fact that Schwarzenegger is not religious and has liberal views on much that the right wing abhors had no importance. The "religious" aspect of the strategy established by the Powell Doctrine in 1971, from which the right wing has never deviated, is purely utilitarian: pander to the fundamentalist churches and get them to pick up the slack as the federal social safety net is destroyed, ensuring that the poor who depend on the churches for services such as abuse counseling, homeless shelters, loans to start small businesses, and free meals will not only vote, as they customarily don't, but vote in what has become their own best interest—the party that promises to help fund church-based activities.

As for Schwarzenegger's liberal support for stem cell research, a woman's right to choose, legal gay unions, and other such important matters, one enthralled woman delegate at the RNC, questioned on this very topic immediately after Schwarzenegger's convention speech, told a reporter, "I think if I had a nice long chat with him I could change his mind about abortion."

Well, she couldn't, in fact, because Arnold Schwarzenegger really does believe in a woman's right to choose, the civil rights of homosexuals, and the need for stem cell research, and Schwarzenegger, once he acquires a belief, never changes his mind about anything. (Anything, that is, that doesn't threaten to get in his way. I am not suggesting that his beliefs are matters of deep conviction: he's more comfortable, perhaps, in what neoconservatives view as a "permissive" culture, but at the moment any belief becomes an obstacle to Schwarzenegger's current ambition, he discards it and "believes" something else. The private behavior of the powerful has never at all conformed with whatever "morality" they impose on the Many; Schwarzenegger wants power much more than he wants a society that shares his personal behavioral comfort zone.) If you listened carefully to his speech at the RNC, Schwarzenegger became a Republican in the first place because, before he even knew much English, he watched a speech Richard Nixon gave on television in 1968.

The RNC audience, I believe, interpreted this moment in Schwarzenegger's speech—the one truly unexpected thing that came out of his mouth—as an apparently long-awaited vindication of the party's most thoroughly disgraced past president, and it elicited the most frenzied applause. Even the ecstatic delegates looked startled as they cheered, since Nixon's very name had been carefully avoided in any Republican convention address since 1975.

It's hardly paradoxical that a rehabilitated Nixon remains a Nixon whose domestic and diplomatic policies were far to the left of those of either party's 2004 presidential candidate, and more like Schwarzenegger than George W. Bush: there is the party, and then there are the party's internally competing interests. As long as the party holds power, the government it controls can be shifted in one direction or another without the annoying formalities of the democratic process.

This, of course, began to backfire as of November 2004, within weeks of Bush's election. (We really cannot call it "re-election.") The elements of the Republican Party who perceived an advantage in using Christianity as an implement have made the grave mistake of actually promoting fundamentalist Christian candidates for public office, who are now numerous enough in Congress to dispense with George Bush and his agenda. For all his incessantly iterated piety—genuine, but only insofar as he thanks Jesus for getting him off booze and out of bankruptcy—Bush is a dedicated member of the Property Party and not the Apocalypse Party of the Rapture. The Rapture is going way too far for the Property Party, since property itself will become non-existent when the Rapture comes along.

And so, paradoxically, the only hope of the Republican Party to survive is to become the Schwarzenegger and Nixon Party—that is, Rockefeller Republicans—while the Democrats perceive their only hope in becoming more like the Rapture Party. Perhaps, in our lifetimes, we will see the Republicans become once again the party of Abraham Lincoln, and the Democrats the party of the Dixiecrats.

THREE

The scope of Arnold Schwarzenegger's ambition has been noted since his first blush of last-name celebrity. (During his dubious feather-plucking days, he was simply identified as "Arnold," and in the credits of *Hercules in New York* as "Arnold Strong.") On the set of *Stay Hungry,* in 1975, he told photographer Roberta Neiman, "Someday I'm going to be president of the United States" (Anne Louise Bardach, "Taming the Hydra-Headed Carnivorous Beast," *Los Angeles Magazine*, September, 2004).

If there was little to conjure the visions of Camelot, manufactured by Jacqueline Kennedy after her husband's assassination, in the 1986 marriage of a walking gymnasium and a skeletally emaciated, secondary member of the Kennedy clan, Schwarzenegger's wedding to Maria Shriver did reflect the easy fusion of politics and show business in the pop heart and mind.

Not too many years earlier, it had seemed absurd that Schwarzenegger could become a movie star, even of the laconic, expressionless type like Clint Eastwood or Gary Cooper, who really could act and used impassivity to that end. It was easier to picture Jean-Claude van Damme, Sylvester Stallone, or even Steven

Seagal as a screen idol action figure: movie stars are sexually charged figures, and Schwarzenegger has never emitted any sort of sexual allure on screen.

James Cameron's casting of Schwarzenegger in *The Terminator* made Arnold a major movie star—and, had it not been for *The Terminator*'s unexpected success and its appeal to both a pop audience and serious film writers who found in it what is, in fact, a very rich mythic subtext, Schwarzenegger's film career might easily have become what Jean-Claude van Damme's has, without the sex appeal. *Terminator* established a persona that was not only bankable but a bulletproof draw for a ticket audience far bigger than Arnold's demographic of adolescent males whose sexual energies tend to fixate on advanced weaponry, explosions, and narratives of mechanical simplicity.

It also seemed ponderous, before the Kennedy connection, that the Austrian Oak (as he had often been billed in his body-building days) could strike millions as a plausible candidate for public office. The Kennedy family, however, despite its misfortunes, its hereditary satyriasis, its scandals, and its origins in bootlegging during Prohibition, was still held to represent the vestige of respectable and powerful liberalism and "ideals," in the manner of a powerful consortium; its extended clan gathered in "compounds," like Shakespearean royals in their many castles. The birthdays of Rose Kennedy occasioned media encomiums appropriate to the Queen Mother of England.

To share family holidays with the Kennedys implied not only membership in an exclusive and rarefied power circle, but access to the secret mechanisms of power, techniques of political image-manipulation, and, most significantly, highly developed techniques of damage control and crisis management.

By 1991, publications such as the *Columbia Journalism Review* were charting Schwarzenegger's political trajectory and citing potential obstacles to its prospects. The first of the latter was a book by Wendy Leigh, *Arnold: An Unauthorized Biography*. The degree of revelation in Leigh's book is fractional. Its subject is not, for example, exposed as having committed a felony or having done anything one could consider vastly worse than things he'd already admitted doing.

What was unusual, to the *CJR* and many other publications, were the unusual lengths to which Schwarzenegger and his associates went to suppress Leigh's book and block its publication, and, after failing that, to interfere with its promotion.

Leigh's book simply documents a history of loose sexual behavior and some peculiarly favorable statements about Adolf Hitler—considering that Schwarzenegger has said on many occasions that he has always hated everything that Hitler represented, if "always" has the same meaning for him as it does for most people—and mentions that Schwarzenegger's father, the police chief of Graz during the Nazi period, applied for membership in the Nazi Party in 1938 and persisted in his efforts until being admitted to the party a few years later.

Leigh reported that Gustav Schwarzenegger "was an alcoholic who raised his two sons, Arnold and Meinhard, as bullies who delighted in publicly humiliating friends as well as rivals." (In *Pumping Iron,* early Arnold candidly relates his techniques for humiliating his best friend, fellow competitor Franco Columbo); as governor, and at the Republican National Convention, he referred to his opposition in the Sacramento legislature and to the Democratic opposition to George Bush, respectively, as "girlie men"—a misogynist bully's insult to other heterosexual men, widely and erroneously interpreted as an expression of homophobia.

Leigh also revealed Arnold's uninhibited use of anabolic steroids during his bodybuilding career, somewhat less of a transgression than the author seemed to consider it. He was not, after all, competing in the Olympics or any actual sport, but engaging in an activity devoted entirely to self-display. Nevertheless, habitual steroid use has been accepted in courts of law as a cause for temporary insanity resulting in homicide.

Everything Leigh recounted about Schwarzenegger in her book could be expediently chalked up to guilt by association, youthful silliness, or behavior that harmed no one but himself. Yet for a subject with his eye on a much more attainable goal than even his run for the governorship of California years after her book appeared, it was sufficiently threatening that Leigh reported receiving menacing late-night telephone calls during the course of her research; her publisher reported receiving offers for a different book by Schwarzenegger himself in exchange for suppressing Leigh's book; the publisher's offices were broken into four times in a single month while the book was in production.

When *Arnold: An Unauthorized Biography* saw print, Leigh's promotional bookings on TV and feature articles about it in print media were abruptly canceled. Schwarzenegger sued the author for libel in Britain, where libel laws are notoriously elastic and far more inclusively defined than those in the United States. (In Britain, even the dead can sue for libel.)

These manifestations were beyond the most aggressive damage control any film star would attempt. Schwarzenegger never viewed becoming a film star as anything other than a means to an end, in any case. In the October 1985 issue of *Interview,* Arnold said: "I never think about money. I don't. I don't like that whole idea of being into money. I like to make good money only because it's part of the game. You have to have a certain value in Hollywood. There's the $5,000 actor, the $1 million actor, $5 million actor, and so on. You have a certain value, so you try to put yourself higher and higher up into this category."

A year after the *Columbia Journalism Review* article, *Spy* magazine amplified on the Wendy Leigh affair. In the English libel suit, then still unresolved, Schwarzenegger's lawyers offered a pre-publication "settlement" that required a substantial cash payment to Schwarzenegger, along with Leigh's promise to "exclude material dealing with 'Arnold's homosexual experiences, his use of steroids, his sale of steroids, his theft of automobiles or his involvement in passport forgery." According to *Spy*, Schwarzenegger's attorneys "just brought [these activities] up entirely out of the blue." As there is nothing in Leigh's book, which appeared without any tampering from Arnold's legal representatives, referring to his *sale* of steroids, his homosexual *experiences,* car theft, or passport forgery, at least two of these preemptively assumed items had never entered Leigh's research to begin with, nor had they been alleged or hinted at anywhere else that I have been able to discover. So it's odd, to say the least, that the latter two, specific felony crimes, would be something thrown in at random to cover all contingent discoveries.

The *Spy* story identified Franco Columbo—Schwarzenegger's best friend and former workout partner, the one he so candidly described bullying and humiliating in the interview portions of *Pumping Iron*—and "either Joe or Ben Weider" as the "associates" who had offered Leigh's publisher "either a large amount of money or a biography written with Arnold" in exchange for killing Leigh's book. One of the book's publicists told the magazine that Arnold and his PR person at the time, Charlotte Parker, "did everything in their power to make Leigh's life miserable. . . . She didn't get on certain shows that Arnold had power over." (*Spy* quoted two reporters as describing Parker as "the most loathed woman in Hollywood.")

Spy and *CJR* shared with Wendy Leigh an almost touching faith in the general reader's powers of inference. One could say it would have been unusual if someone born in Bavaria in 1947 had a father who *hadn't* belonged to the Nazi Party, though not everyone's was so eager to join that he persisted for several years in seeking membership; and, indeed, it would have been extraordinary for anyone to hold the Mr. Universe title for six consecutive years *without* using anabolic steroids.

By early 2001, Arnold Schwarzenegger was actively exploring his chances of becoming the Republican candidate for governor of California in a general election. There was little to stop him except his own reputation. He already had Pete Wilson and his team prepping him for the avalanche of dirty laundry that would come out if Schwarzenegger had any, and of course he did.

Schwarzenegger's own team of muscle impresarios had failed to squash Wendy Leigh's book, but had been fairly successful in sabotaging its promotion. But neither the Columbo-Weider clan nor the Wilson strategy nerds anticipated the March 2001 issue of *Premiere* magazine and its lead story by John Connolly, "Arnold the Barbarian."

Connolly's piece documented precisely the kinds of damning information the *Los Angeles Times* later re-investigated or discovered on its own:

> Anna Richardson of Big Screen claims that after the cameras stopped rolling for her interview segment, Schwarzenegger . . . tweaked her nipple and then laughed at her objections. "What was more upsetting was that his people rushed up to protect him and scapegoated me, and not one person came to apologize afterwards."
>
> During the production of . . . *Terminator 2* . . . a producer on that film recalls Arnold emerging from his trailer . . . and noticing a fortyish female crew member. . . . Arnold went up to the woman, put his hands inside her blouse, and proceeded to pull her breasts out of her bra. Another observer says: "I couldn't believe what I was seeing. This woman's nipples were exposed, and here's Arnold and a few of his clones laughing . . . she . . . refused to press charges for fear of losing her job. It was disgusting.
>
> A female producer . . . tells of a time when her ex-husband came to visit the set. When she introduced the man to Schwarzenegger, the star quipped, "Is this guy the reason why you didn't come up to my hotel room last night and suck my cock?"

There were many such incidents reported by Connolly, as well as certain medical information, confirmed by named physicians and other people in a position to know, indicating that

Schwarzenegger's defective heart valve could not be replaced in the usual way because of his long, excessive use of steroids; and further revelations about the star's fanatical hypervigilance over his image. He had even canned his semi-feral pit bull of a publicist for failing to suppress a story about one of his infidelities.

At roughly the same time the March issue of *Premiere* hit the stands, the tabloids, for which Arnold was regular grist for the mill, ran similar stories: "Arnold's Shocking 7-Year Affair," "Arnold's Dirty Secrets—Why He Can't Run for Governor," and the like.

But then something unusual happened, reversing Schwarzenegger's run of ill luck. It happened that the success of more mainstream "life among the rich and famous" lifestyle magazines had eaten into the tabloid market considerably years earlier; Rupert Murdoch, who owned the *Star,* dumped it as a bad deal onto Boston Ventures, which then became American Media, Inc. AMI, over the course of the 1990s, acquired all the profitable tabloids in America.

AMI's three-story headquarters for all its tabloid publishing at 5401 Broken Sound Boulevard in Boca Raton, Florida, had been recently renovated, boosting the property's value to $20 million. On October 5, 2001, AMI photo editor Bob Stevens died of anthrax exposure. He was probably the first person exposed, and definitely the first to die, from the still unsolved anthrax attacks that followed the suicide attacks on New York and Washington on September 11.

There has never been any proven link between the 9/11 events and the anthrax letters. Law enforcement entities across the board have speculated that the anthrax letters had no credible relationship to the 9/11 plot, but were the work of domestic, right-wing terrorists. Strange to tell, the subsequent anthrax letters sent to ABC News, CBS News, NBC News, and the *New York Post* all contained notes warning their recipients to "take penacilin [*sic*] now," and the strain of anthrax sent to them was never virulent enough to cause death. The letters sent to Senators Daschle of South Dakota (defeated in November 2004 by a Republican opponent in a re-election contest) and Patrick Leahy of Vermont (the Patrick Leahy whom Vice President Cheney advised to "go fuck himself" on the Senate floor), on the other hand, contained "weaponized" anthrax, as did the letter received by the hapless Mr. Stevens.

Many other AMI employees subsequently tested positive for anthrax exposure. The building on Broken Sound Boulevard was sealed, and its entire photo library and archives were declared contaminated and had to be destroyed.

Florida governor Jeb Bush, who made it his business to visit every site of an anthrax attack in the South, pointedly ignored the one site where someone had actually died, never expressed the slightest sympathy for Mr. Stevens's grieving family or co-workers, and refused to let the state award a single penny to AMI. The tabloids had, you see, reported the drug problems and arrest for "sexual misconduct" of Jeb Bush's children Noelle and Jebby, respectively, and their sibling George P. Bush, who broke into his girlfriend's house after tearing up her lawn with his car.

David Pecker, AMI's CEO, was offered three options by a spokesperson for Senator Bill Nelson of Florida. He could sell the building to the government for $1. The government would clean it, then sell it and keep the profits. Or the government would help with the cleanup and ship the building's contents to

Ft. Detrick Army Base in Maryland for disposal. Or the government could turn the site into a laboratory for anthrax studies.

Faced with massive loss of revenues, AMI sold the building to a company owned by one David Rustine for $40,000. Rustine then hired Bio-ONE, a joint venture company, teaming Sabre Technical Services, "a leader in biological and chemical remediation technology" with Giuliani Partners, "a management and consulting firm with extensive experience in security, emergency preparedness and response, as well as crisis management," whose CEO was, is, former New York mayor Rudolph W. Giuliani. The headquarters of this new joint venture company? Well, none other than the detoxified AMI Building.

Another of life's little ironies, apparently.

David Pecker of AMI, in 2002, at a cost of $350 million, acquired the Weider Publications Group, which published seven magazines, mostly devoted to bodybuilding and men's fitness, and was part of a business empire that encompassed something called Weider Nutrition, which had been marketing the steroid ephedra to bodybuilders for years, and also owned Schiff vitamins.

It happens, of course, that the Weider conglomerate was founded by Joe Weider, the impresario who brought Arnold Schwarzenegger to our shores from Austria in the late 1960s. Weider's brother Ben operated the company's International Federation of Bodybuilders. Arnold Schwarzenegger had officially endorsed Weider Nutrition's products and held a significant interest in Weider stock.

It further happens that the magazines acquired by Weider from AMI were heavily dependent upon Arnold Schwarzenegger's participation. And that Weider persuaded Pecker to give Arnold 10 percent of AMI as their mutual publicist.

After these deals were worked out to everyone's financial satisfaction, negative stories about Arnold Schwarzenegger disappeared from AMI's tabloids. The *Globe,* the *Star,* the *National Enquirer,* and the *Weekly World News,* in fact, became rabid boosters of Schwarzenegger's campaign for governor.

I really don't know what, if anything, to conclude from this bizarre sequence of events, though political damage control has been known to extend into some funny areas, depending on your sense of humor.

In a culture of victimhood and recuperation such as ours, a "wound culture" where a sense of community is generated exclusively by disasters and scandals, Schwarzenegger's "negatives" would logically suggest at least something worth further investigation; yet instead, the plethora of sexual obtusities, the steroid abuse, and other such items reported before the election lent themselves more readily to "positive" narratives of redemption favored by Christian fundamentalists: he said he was sorry if he offended anybody, said it just so, humble-like, elbowing inconvenient bits of the past out of his way, and his sparkling dental work evoked the narrative of the abused child who rose by his own will above a devastating background, the narrative of the self-made immigrant who learned from his early mistakes, and so forth. People "liked" Arnold, as people were said to "like" George Bush, and that settled that.

So there was this, too: political discourse, the parsing of issues, the actual intent of a potential candidate for high public office had become matters of such indifference that the public, and the candidate, and the press that reported on the candidate, viewed questions of the public good as entirely peripheral to "a perception or emotion" that described "the total experience of having a relationship" with the candidate.

The total experience of having a relationship with Arnold Schwarzenegger that many people believed they had, and its transference from the world of make-believe into the arena of government, spoke to the possibility that the democratic experiment was rapidly mutating into a ceremonial fantasy.

Governor Schwarzenegger's rapturous reception at the RNC dramatized the surreal extent to which public reality had blurred into entertainment, the dispensations of fiction spilling into the realm of facts.

The larger themes of Schwarzenegger's speech, and, for that matter, the persona he had projected into the world, were in perfect alignment with the militarism and xenophobia the Bush II administration had skillfully mobilized after the 9/11 attacks. (More curiously, and tellingly, he personified and was admired for the same qualities by Islamic fanatics in places like Iran and Algeria, by the dictator of North Korea, and in many parts of the world where America itself was despised for its foreign policy and flagrant hypocrisy. Indeed, anywhere brutality and violence are everyday facts of life, Schwarzenegger's films are even more popular than they are in the United States.)

Schwarzenegger presented himself at the RNC as the incarnation of American superiority, the living evidence that "working hard and playing by the rules"—whatever those were—could take a person anywhere in freedom's land. Standard fare, but Arnold had chosen America as home, over Europe—specifically, a part of the "old Europe" the secretary of defense had lately singled out as a superannuated relic, as opposed to the "new Europe"—Spain, Poland, Costa Rica, the Micronesian Islands, and many other nominally sovereign countries—that had joined the "coalition" to invade Iraq (from which Costa Rica, though it had never committed actual troops but ever-mindful of its dependence on the tourist industry, was among the first of many to withdraw, with Spain and Poland following its lead at a more protracted pace). Arnold resurrected the specter of Communism and the moral aporias of the Cold War by burnishing his own history with wild hyperbole no nativist politician could have convincingly pulled off. It was propaganda in the service of narcissism, one of many skills that George W. Bush himself had barely developed beyond the most rudimentary and obvious level. Schwarzenegger had refined it, with all the resources of Hollywood long before, into an effective tool, something like a jackhammer that produced a noise no more annoying than the wheeze of a dental drill in somebody else's mouth.

"The Soviets occupied part of Austria. I saw their tanks in the street. I saw communism with my own eyes . . . as a kid I saw the socialist country that Austria became after the Soviets left."

The cunning European peasant youth who reads the world around him exclusively in terms of obstacles to his own advancement is a cherished figure of American immigrant mythology. It's easy to credit such a youth's fear "that the soldiers would pull my father or uncle out of the car, and I'd never see them again."

Even if you found the general drift of this speech appalling, only a heart of stone would fail to hear the ring of authenticity, especially a heart that grew up during the Cold War. That is, a heart unattached to a brain that didn't know that Styria, the Austrian province where Schwarzenegger grew up, was occupied after World War II by the Allies, and that there never existed more than a few Soviet tanks anywhere in postwar Austria, least of all Styria. (Austria was, in fact, the only country from which the Soviets voluntarily withdrew after being awarded it at the Yalta Conference.) Or that between the date of Schwarzenegger's birth in 1947 through 1968, the year he came to our shores, every Austrian chancellor was a conservative, and the country run by coalition governments.

Ronald Reagan, of course, had vividly remembered helping to liberate Nazi concentration camps in Europe, though he had never left Hollywood during World War II. He'd also once famously observed that "facts are stupid things," which has become more than ever the reigning dictum of the faith-based Republican Party.

The breastified male is neither Greek nor antediluvian. It originates in comic books and adventure magazines of the 1930s and 1940s. The pasts of Conan the Barbarian, Red Sonja, and other Schwarzeneggerian characters are a pastiche of the Mongol Empire, the Rome of Tiberius, Arthurian legends, and the planet Krypton. In this amalgam, which is arguably the "prehistory" of the world as imagined by Creationists (who now have their own myth of origin posted as an alternative to the geological, scientific facts in our national parks and places like the Grand Canyon), women achieve personhood by becoming warriors—in other words, men—while the harsh exertions of men equip them with breasts, usurping one of the biological functions of women.

In *Junior*, Schwarzenegger takes this process a significant step further—not with any originality, as a much better elaboration of the same idea was written and directed decades ago by Joan

Rivers—when an embryo is implanted in Arnold's abdomen by his frequent comedy partner, Danny DeVito, as a research experiment. Arnold becomes the world's first pregnant man. The "baby" is supposed to be—well, terminated, so to speak, long before the end of the first trimester, but Arnold develops, hormonally, protective maternal instincts, develops the stereotyped behavior of a pregnant mom-to-be, and refuses to abort it. He carries the fetus to term. He gives birth to a child originating in one of Emma Thompson's fertilized eggs. He becomes, in other words, the first entirely self-sufficient human being.

It is 1977. A milky vapor shaped like a spermatozoon looms in the night above Vatican City. A priest viewing this vapor from a window briskly removes a gold-ornamented, bible-shaped casket from an important desk drawer. Inside, numerous centuries-old metal cylinders preserve rolls of prophetic ancient offset lithographs helpful in identifying portents of supernatural cataclysm. The priest immediately unscrolls this divinely inspired papyrus to confirm his lowering surmise that a comet depicted in one especially nasty pictorial omen is virtually identical to the bright smear visible above the moon—indubitably an omen, as it isn't streaking through the heavens, as ordinary comets are known to do, but loitering in a fixed position, like something you'd find in a prophetic ancient offset lithograph.

The priest hurries through the magnificently appointed Vatican palace in that little black cassock suitable for evening wear and casual occasions alike, climbing many marble stairways, bustling across gigantic empty spaces under vaulted ceilings. At the base of a final staircase, he sweeps past a matching set of Swiss Guards and breathlessly enters an ecclesiastical lounging area of epic dimensions, its decor favoring muted conservative colors but visibly priceless beyond reckoning. There, the local faculty of the College of Cardinals is ranged about on luscious leather furniture, at an appropriately cringing remove from an elevated but unremarkable armchair, where an austere figure all in white, unmistakably the Pope, learns that the comet known among Vatican hoi polloi as "the eye of God" has appeared.

It's not indicated whether this group has assembled in anticipation of this dread inevitability, or simply dropped in for coffee. It is, of course, an established fact that the Pope, in all his film roles, never budges from his throne or chair, too burdened by his tragic foreknowledge of any world-threatening unpleasantness. He's no stranger to the eye of God and what its appearance in the heavens portends, to say the least.

Once in a thousand years, the eye of God hovers like a bleached Romanian eyebrow in the sky. At that exact moment a female child is born on earth, bearing a birthmark shaped like the Greek character omega or a nasty insect bite. It is foretold that the Evil One will mate with this omega woman when she reaches childbearing age, and their postcoital tryst after conceiving the Anti-Christ will usher in the End of Days.

This doomed infant must be found, certainly before she hits puberty. Everybody's copacetic with that, but what to do with her afterwards raises such bickering that soon it will divide the confusingly profuse branches of the Catholic hierarchy into rival gangs.

The Pope, an actor familiar to me because we often reside in the same Los Angeles hotel, is urged by a stocky, bearded cardinal to have the child killed as soon as she's discovered. They all know she's the only one who can bear His child, and that will spell curtains for all creation. (Curiously, whenever He or Him is audibly capitalized in this kind of film, the pronoun refers to Satan rather than the deity.)

Sacrifice an innocent child? Is the Pope Catholic? The Bishop of Rome and Vicar of Jesus Christ, Primate of Italy and Successor of St. Peter will have none of it: murdering a child would almost be worse than aborting a fetus. Find the girl, absolutely, but "we must protect her," the Pontiff insists, causing the infanticide faction to boil in grim silence.

It is 1999. Mere days before the millennium. On a Manhattan avenue, some sort of gas explosion knocks building pediments into the street and causes geysers of fire to spew out of manholes. Meanwhile, a sort of transparent oil slick, momentarily resembling a winged satanic gargoyle but instantly subsiding into a shapeless undulating ripple, whisks through the city like rubbing alcohol or a virulent brand of odorless aftershave. It sweeps into a pricey restaurant where a suave businessman played by Gabriel Byrne is seated with friends. He excuses himself to visit the men's room. After a piss, he's seized by the transparent goo, thrown against the wall, and knocked all over the restroom. After extensive mauling, Byrne is "taken over" by the Evil One.

The following morning Jericho, the protagonist, is first seen groping around for a gun in an empty pizza box and pressing its business end into his forehead. Droplets of sweat suggest that despair and suicidal impulses are Jericho's only abiding companions. Jericho works for a security company. His partner fortuitously raps at the apartment door before Jericho can end it all.

Their mission that day involves guarding a rich client while he conducts some unidentified business. Jericho asks who the guy is. "Some Wall Street scumbag."

Jericho, so tired of life that food is nothing to him except fuel, throws every edible scrap in the apartment together in a blender and gulps the repulsive, macerated gunk.

"I like scumbags," he says as a cynical taunt. "They pay better."

The scumbag, who seems to require a convoy of stretch limousines, an array of snipers perched on rooftops, and an emergency helicopter simply to visit an ATM, turns out to be the now Luciferian Gabriel Byrne. We never learn who he previously was, and the question never arises. Byrne's body hasn't merely been occupied by the devil; he is the devil, with myriad supernatural powers, including physical invulnerability. (Why an indestructible person needs the services of a security firm is one of this movie's least provoking idiocies, which really tells you something.) Jericho—who spends the remainder of the film swiftly piecing together the End of Days thing through his own supernatural powers of deduction and protecting Christine, the girl born under a comet, from sexual penetration by the Evil One—is, of course, played by Arnold Schwarzenegger.

The Schwarzenegger character's backstory has a familiarly blocky, mechanistic unreality: wife and small daughter brutally murdered in the middle past, consequent repudiation of God, sole remaining interest in life solving crimes and avenging evil, morally challenged by his own bitterness. After rescuing Christine from several rape attempts by Satan, attempted murder by a veritable platoon of renegade Jesuits, and assault by the girl's evil stepmother—the very plump nurse who spirited her from her real mother's arms immediately after her birth into the hospital basement where Udo Kier baptized her in snake blood!—despite mounting evidence that demonic forces beyond his powers of belief are stalking Christine for the express purpose of making her fuck the devil before midnight on December 31, 1999—the expiration date on Satan's sperm, apparently—Jericho nevertheless rejects the protection offered Christine by the pastor of a modest little Catholic church which contains a powerful, virtually Satan-proof spiritual force field. This pastor is not merely an authority on the End of Days and a veteran thwarter of Evil far better equipped than Jericho to keep Christine's cherry intact until the midnight hour—he's Rod Steiger!

As the clock ticks, Gabriel Byrne beams himself into Jericho's apartment like a nasty hologram and tempts him just as Christ was tempted in the desert, conjuring up happy Christmas moments Jericho spent with his slain family, offering to reverse time and create an alternative future in which Jericho's wife and daughter are still alive. When that fails, he recreates every sensory detail of their murders. We, too, see every gory moment. Jericho's grimacing struggle against The Adversary (who, being Gabriel Byrne, cuts a more elegant and appealing figure than the pathetic mess Jericho has become), his rictus of grief and anger at the sight of the mayhem that has ruined his life, pretty well covers the range of Schwarzenegger's expressivity. There are deeper reasons for this than a shortage of talent, but first let's wrap up this synopsis.

Briefly, after encountering direct proof of the reality of Hell and therefore the existence of God, Jericho entrusts Christine to the Church of Rod Steiger. Unfortunately, this refuge proves insufficiently bathed in blessed rays to keep the original fallen angel from busting in. First the sacred environs of the altar are

invaded by marauding cardinals and bishops intent on euthaniz-
ing Christine with a consecrated dagger, then the building
shakes and rattles like a stilt-supported dingbat at the epicenter
of the Northridge earthquake. Jericho saves Christine from the
homicidal clergymen, but Gabriel Byrne shows up simultaneously, indifferent to the many representations of Christ all about,
like the garlic-and-crucifix-immune undead in Roman Polan-
ski's *Dance of the Vampires*.

Most of the malignant church officials and several benign
ones as well get slaughtered in the ensuing free-for-all. If this
isn't bad enough, Jericho's security company chum has been
zombie-ized and abducts Christine while Satan crucifies Jericho
in an alley beside the church. Fortunately no nails are on hand,
so Jericho is merely roped to an I-beam and menaced by a mob
of hell-bent psychos who have been "taken over." They dis-
perse, however, to catch Christine's impregnation, which Satan
has booked into a boarded-up Keith Circuit vaudeville hall.
Rod Steiger and several miraculously not-dead colleagues un-
crucify Jericho, who scrambles to intercept the conception of
the Antichrist.

And so on. Perhaps the most revelatory scene, as far as our
subject is concerned, occurs at the penultimate moment before a
toilet of swirling antimatter, synchronized with Eastern Daylight
Savings Time, is scheduled to suck Satan back to Hell like a
flushed turd for another thousand years, in the absence of "completion." The ball in Times Square, in fact, has started its descent
when the devil dematerializes into the clear watery whatever he
arrived as, and though he's running out of seconds to penetrate
Christine, he does the diabolically next best thing and funnels
himself into Arnold Schwarzenegger.

We are, once again, in a church, and the ten-megaton urge of Jericho's inner Beelzebub to hump the exhausted heroine wars with his co-inhabitive, recovered monotheism. The clash of two Arnolds in one Schwarzenegger tops all the film's earlier mayhem—spurting severed arteries, graphic decapitations, stabbings, incinerations, gunshot fatalities, eviscerations, and explosions—chewing up a spectacular effulgence of Savior-minded art direction, including a De Mille–scale Jesus on the Cross.

The boilerplate and its contemptuous disdain for any human motivation more ambivalent or less imperative than the survival instinct is a common feature of Arnold Schwarzenegger's movies; what's uncommon, widely admired, narcotically seductive, and scary is Arnold Schwarzenegger's embrace and embodiment, in real life, of the homiletic conventions, phobic rejection of cerebral nuance, and authoritarian ideology his films transmit through a camouflage of winking ironies and seemingly uninhibited self-parody.

He has never been an actor playing a character; in Schwarzenegger's roles, the character plays him (or more precisely, the physical sculpture of his public image, and the biographical narrative that becomes "him" between its frequent revisions). The fictional Schwarzenegger hero incarnates the bodybuilder-turned-actor-turned-governor's reductive view of politics, morality, and social relations, enacts his messianic fantasies, dramatizes his fierce and almost robotic preoccupation with winning and getting his way. The Schwarzenegger character ennobles an oxymoronic "sensitive machismo" by projecting it into prehistories of rampant barbarism, pitting it against present-day villainy, engaging it in epic future battle against some technological menace or apocalyptic spiritual struggle.

Even within its own narrative premises, *End of Days* is a film of unlimited incoherence and crudity, but it exemplifies what the archetype-cliché Arnold Schwarzenegger embodies in the culture of images, and the messages his persona and vast celebrity convey to the citizen-consumer in what can credibly be termed post-democratic America.

FOUR

The California recall offered a choice opportunity for general resentment to play itself out as theater. Thirty-four previous efforts to recall a sitting California government had never gotten beyond the petition stage. Governor Gray Davis's approval numbers, however, had plunged from 66 percent in 2000 to 22 percent in mid-2003: enough slippage, at last, that 1.7 million voters were willing to put a special election on the table.

The move to recall Davis was launched, immediately after his re-election, by Ted Costa, chieftain of People's Advocate, an anti-tax and anti-government group operating from a small office behind a Krispy Kreme donut franchise in a Sacramento strip mall. Costa viewed the recall as a perfect opportunity for Arnold Schwarzenegger's long-festering dream of political power.

People's Advocate, characterized by one Democratic consultant as "a blood-sucking institution," was founded by the late Paul Gann. It is famed for initiating Proposition 13, also known as the Jarvis Amendment, a ballot initiative that became California law in 1978.

Prop. 13 immediately devastated California's tax base by cutting $7 billion in property taxes. Proposition 4, a follow-up measure, dramatically cut spending increases for educational and social services. Another People's Advocate measure, the "Victim's Bill of Rights," stiffened criminal sentences well beyond the usual understanding of the term "cruel and unusual punishment," effectively transforming "twenty-five to life" into "life without parole," multiplying the state's incarcerated population and thereby enhancing the awesome power of the prison guards union, the most powerful lobbying group in Sacramento.

People's Advocate is the kind of "grass-roots organization" skilled at appealing to working-class voters whose actual best interests it diametrically opposes, essentially servicing the affluent, nativist, white Californian population. It has an illustrious record matched only by the history of Tammany Hall. Proposition 13, for example, was made attractive to non–property owners by offering tenant rent rollbacks; it contained a loophole for landlords who made cosmetic improvements to their rental properties which, as per the statute, qualified as structural renovations just prior to Prop. 13's passage. In the vernacular of the grift, People's Advocate specializes in the short con.

Other recall players included Howard Kaloogian, a state assemblyman, and Sal Russo, a right-wing consultant, who launched a Web site where Internet users could download the recall petition. Talk radio fastened on the recall idea, its drive-time demagogues whipping up a sense of impending crisis on every freeway in California.

The state's budget deficit was a standard theme, its amount invariably inflated from the "out-year problem" of $8 billion left out of that year's balanced budget to $38 billion. Meanwhile, the average family home had appreciated by $100,000 in 2003. Unemployment was well short of the national average.

Pro-recall radio hosts—an overwhelming majority—fueled this manufactured anger of the well-off with the specter of illegal immigrants obtaining driver's licenses and the reality of a 2 percent increase in vehicle registration fees mandated by legislation passed by Gray Davis's predecessor, Republican Pete Wilson.

The racist tone of Sacramento's Eric Hogue and San Diego's Roger Hedgecock was unmistakable, and only slightly more rabid than that of dozens of other radio drones. John and Ken, a statewide-syndicated pair of clowns, referred to Gray Davis as "a rotting stool that ought to be flushed." The deficit was blamed squarely, cent for cent, on undocumented aliens, whose access to social services had already been slashed by ballot initiatives.

The world beyond California did not understand the recall. Neither did most Californians. For better or worse, the enabling statutes had existed since 1911, originating from a progressive reform movement.

The early history of white California, for many people, amounts to a handful of hazily apprehended events: the Mexican War, the Donner party incident, "the railroad," the Gold Rush, and, perhaps, the Great Frisco Quake and the Dust Bowl migration. Throw in Tate-LaBianca and Altamont and you've really said it all, from an East Coast point of view. Outside California, the state is often depicted as a vortex of bizarre religious cults and "alternative lifestyles," with half its laterite shelf sliding into the Pacific and the other half oscillating between right- and left-wing fanaticism.

In reality, California is like the rest of America, only more so. (Most of its notable utopian experiments and crackpot religions originated in western and upstate New York.) Like America itself, California has always been the filter on a giant human drain, collecting bits of everything that's washed through it during the national expansion we owe to Manifest Destiny and the nation's economic shifts.

What is unusual in California is a pattern of development directly at odds with geography. California has been thickly settled according to the logic of the long con, in deserts requiring endless artificial irrigation, along active earthquake fault lines, in conformity with land grabs and real estate scams.

For much of the nineteenth century, the railroad brought everything in and moved everything through California to the Pacific coast. The Southern Pacific brokered the state's political power for much of the nineteenth century. The railroad's original charter extended from San Francisco into Southern California, to Arizona, New Mexico, and Western Texas; absorbed in 1868 by the Central Pacific, it eventually ran all the way to New Orleans. It built new towns where existing ones refused it right of way; it drove thousands of farmers off its fallow land grants; it established monopolies on freight routes. By the 1880s, the railroad was widely regarded as a public menace rather than a utility.

The accidental presidency of Theodore Roosevelt after McKinley's assassination in 1901 produced a reform movement that eventually brought the economic insanity of the Gilded Age to an end. Roosevelt beefed up the Interstate Commerce Act of 1887 with the Elkins Act of 1903, ending the railroad's rebates to oil and livestock companies. This was followed in 1906 by the Hepburn Act, which expanded the Interstate Commerce Commission from five to seven members, giving the ICC power to regulate rates and extending its jurisdiction to terminals, pipelines, ferries, and storage facilities. The Elkins Act also shifted the burden of proof in appeals cases from the ICC to the railroads.

Progressive Republican (yes, there were such, once upon a time) Hiram Johnson's election as governor in 1910 resulted in more far-ranging reforms. His inaugural address posed the question, "How best can the government be made responsive to the people alone?"

"In some form or other nearly every governmental problem that involves the health, the happiness, or the prosperity of the State has arisen, because some private interest has intervened or has sought for its own gain to exploit either the resources or the politics of the state," Johnson observed. "I take it, therefore, that the first duty that is mine to perform is to eliminate every private interest from the government, and to make the public service of the State responsive solely to the people."

Johnson proposed to "give to the people the means by which they may accomplish such other reforms as they desire," by means of "the initiative, the referendum, and the recall." Johnson specifically addressed the railroad question, employer liability law, conservation, county home rule, ballot reform, and a nonpartisan judiciary.

The terms in which the recall were set into California law are remarkably looser than those subsequently adopted in other states. While most such laws require evidence of corruption or criminal behavior in office, California's allows a recall to happen on any grounds whatsoever, or no grounds at all:

Sec. 13. Recall is the power of the electors to remove an elective officer.

> Sec. 14 (a). Recall of a state officer is initiated by delivering to the Secretary of State a petition alleging reason for recall. Sufficiency of reason is not reviewable.

The number of petition signatures required to put a recall election for the governorship on the ballot, 12 percent of the number of votes cast in the previous election, is 8 to 32 percent lower than the percentage required by all other states with such laws, except Montana.

The vote itself is bifurcated. The first, obligatory vote is up or down on the recall itself. The second is a choice among alternative candidates. Section 11381 of the election code stipulates that "no person whose recall is being sought may be a candidate to succeed himself or herself at a recall election." (One couldn't, in other words, vote *for* Davis if one opposed the recall: the recall question was itself a vote for or against Davis, vastly reducing the number of majority votes needed for an alternative candidate to win.) Section 11382 invalidates a second vote cast in the absence of a decision on the first vote, eliminating abstention on the recall question itself.

The petition circulated in 2003 did cite reasons for removing Gray Davis, though each had an expedient, nebulous relationship to cause and effect:

> Gross mismanagement of California finances by overspending taxpayers' money, threatening public safety by cutting funds to local governments, failing to account for the exorbitant cost of the energy fiasco, and failing in general to deal with the state's major problems until

they get to the crisis stage. California should not have to be known as the state with poor schools, traffic jams, outrageous utility bills, and huge debts . . . all caused by gross mismanagement.

This is an astonishing paragraph in virtually every detail, and its most overtly absurd item is perhaps its truest reflection of California's special, and specially American, form of pathology. It is a state that pioneered the demonization of the federal government and championed self-reliance while every bit of its development was subsidized by federal grants and subsidies. Its self-reliant agribusiness empire was created entirely by tax exemptions, water rights waivers, and land grants from the federal and state governments. Yet the same organizations and voting blocs that routinely decry all forms of taxation—in a state where the automobile industry has systematically destroyed, in the entire southern half of the state, a once-flourishing public light-rail and electric trolley system to impose a car culture so antithetical to public health and common sense that until emission standards were finally tightened a toxic cloud of smog hung over the entire coastal region from San Diego to somewhere just south of San Francisco—imagine that the state government, or anything, has the magic ability to eliminate traffic jams.

Another digression, quoted from remarks made in Cambridge, Massachusetts, in October 2004 at the Congress for the New Urbanism, New England Chapter, by James Howard Kunstler, may serve to indicate precisely what a short con the pretext for the California recall truly represents, and how empty, consciously or not, Arnold Schwarzenegger's oft-stated belief in the gradual shift to alternative energy sources is:

> Nobody knows when the absolute peak year of global oil production will occur. Some believe we are already at peak and the behavior of the global markets proves it. Saudi Arabia seems to have lost the ability to function as "swing producer." The good news is that OPEC can no longer set the price of oil. The bad news is that nobody can. When there is no production surplus in the world, that's a pretty good sign that the world is at peak.
>
> Princeton geologist Kenneth Deffeyes says that peak production will occur in 2005—that's less than three months away. Others, like Colin Campbell, former chief geologist for Shell Oil, put it more conservatively as between now and 2007.

• • •

The meaning of the oil peak and its enormous implications are generally misunderstood even by those who have heard about it—and this includes mainstream corporate media and the Americans who make plans or policy.

The world does not have to run out of oil or natural gas for severe instabilities, network breakdowns, and systems failures to occur. All that is necessary is for world production capacity to reach its absolute limit—a point at which no increased production is possible and the long arc of depletion commences, with oil production then falling by a few percentages steadily every year thereafter. That's the global oil peak: the end of absolute increased production and beginning of absolute declining production.

• • •

Long before the oil actually depletes we will endure world-shaking political disturbances and economic disruptions. We will see globalism-in-reverse. Globalism was never an "ism," by the way. It was not a belief system. It was a manifestation of the 20-year-final-blowout of cheap oil. Like all economic distortions, it produced economic perversions. It allowed gigantic, predatory organisms like WalMart to spawn and reproduce at the expense of more cellular fine-grained economic communities.

• • •

Right here I am compelled to inform you that the prospects for alternative fuels are poor. . . . There is not going to be a hydrogen economy. The hydrogen economy is a fantasy. We may be able to run a very few things on hydrogen—but we are not going to replace the entire US automobile fleet with hydrogen fuel cells. Nor will we do it with electric cars or natural gas cars. Wind power and solar electric will not produce significant amounts of power within the context of the way we live now.

No combination of alternative fuel systems currently known will allow us to run what we are running, the way we're running it, or even a significant fraction of it.

• • •

Many of my friends and colleagues live in fear of the federal government turning into Big Brother tyranny.

I'm skeptical. Once the permanent global energy crisis really gets underway, the federal government will be lucky if it can answer the phones. Same thing for Microsoft or even Star Market.

The data supporting James Howard Kunstler's remarks quoted above, and the civilizational upheaval it inescapably portends, are undisputed by any of our major energy-producing entities. Within the lifetime of anyone reading this book who lives beyond 2007, the endless economic growth upon which so many "indicators" are believed to reflect something as trivial as the degree of general prosperity—and on which the America we live in now has proliferated into megasuburbs and desert cities that exhausted their meager indigenous aquifer decades ago, every urban cluster reliant on diverted water, on affordable oil, on air conditioning, and on long-distance food delivery and long-term refrigeration—will vanish with catastrophic suddenness.

Regardless of who is governor of California, or for that matter president of the United States, the moment after the point of peak oil production will also be the end of traffic jams in California. (It will, surely, be the end of traffic in California.)

This is no secret to any advanced nation in the world except America, and since its inception the European Union has been planning for the moment of peak oil, beginning with its mass transit systems. Yes, "old Europe." Superannuated Europe. Even much of "new Europe," as it adjusts to the conditions for entry into the EU, is revising its plans for the future accordingly.

This little digression, in fact, fully places all the reasons given for the recall of Governor Davis in the miniaturizing perspective they deserve, but perhaps most directly the problem of horrible traffic jams.

With deafening tub-thumping from talk radio, People's Advocate, Kaloogian and Russo, et al., the petition drive inched forward with tortoise-like momentum. Costa's strategy hinged on a special election. At a few thousand signatures per day, the recall drive, if it did succeed, could only place the issue on the March 2004 national primary ballot, when heavy Democratic turnout would improve Davis's chances of staying in office.

An Arab American member of the U.S. Congress, Darrell Issa, stepped into the breach with a third pro-recall entity called Rescue California in May 2003. Issa had immensely deep pockets, having reaped millions from the car alarm business. He intended to run for governor himself.

Like the other groups, Rescue California numbered among its talking points the state's "negative business climate," a neatly phrased appeal for larger corporate tax breaks. As it happened, Darrell Issa's own company, Directed Electronics, had moved its corporate headquarters to Florida to avoid paying California taxes. This can, of course, be viewed as proof that Issa had first-hand experience of this negative business climate. In any case, he was able to dump his tax savings into the recall movement.

Rescue California hired professional signature-gathering firms and ad time, swiftly yanking the signatures up to 16,000 per day. By announcing his plans early, Issa also became a sidebar issue himself.

Issa's was a kind of success story familiar from novels by James M. Cain and Raymond Chandler. In 1971, while in the army, eighteen-year-old Issa was accused of stealing a car from Sgt. Jay Bergey, who settled the matter out of court. "I confronted Issa," Bergey later said. "I got in his face and threatened to kill him, and magically my car reappeared the next day." Issa was demoted from a bomb squad assignment after an Article 15 hearing on bad conduct and "allegations that he had stolen a fellow soldier's car."

In Ohio, in 1972, Issa was indicted for auto theft. Charges were dropped when the local district attorney decided not to prosecute.

In Michigan, in 1973, Issa was convicted on weapons charges.

In 1980, Issa was again charged with grand theft auto, in San Jose, California. Again, the DA declined to prosecute.

In 1982, Issa took control of Joe Adkin's car alarm company by calling in a $60,000 loan after making verbal promises to allow Adkin several additional weeks to pay it. Without notifying Adkin, Issa went to court the following day and seized his company. Next, he quadrupled the fire insurance on the company's headquarters. He was observed hauling records and computer equipment out of the building a day before it burned to the ground in an arson fire.

Throughout the 1980s and 1990s, Issa drove several competitors out of business with nuisance lawsuits and intimidation, while outsourcing manufacturing jobs to Taiwan. He found time to run and lose a Senate race in 1998. In 2000, he ran, unopposed, for a House seat, at a cost of $1.7 million—the same figure he eventually sank into the recall.

Issa's background in auto theft was obviously useful in becoming a car alarm entrepreneur. His habit of enriching himself at other people's expense, on the other hand, didn't recommend him in any obvious way for the job of governing the world's sixth largest economy. One right-wing columnist referred to Issa's role in the recall effort as that of "a useful idiot."

Aside from a colorful business and military resumé that was, in truth, less unusual than otherwise, Issa's record in Congress appeared unlikely to win crossover Democratic votes, or votes from moderate Republicans. Even most conservative Republicans in California considered Issa rather loathsome because of positive statements he had made on behalf of Hezbollah.

He advocated school prayer, the criminalization of flag-burning, and restrictions on abortion and stem cell research. He strongly advocated offshore oil drilling. He opposed campaign finance reform, malpractice suits against HMOs, and litigation against gun manufacturers. After 9/11, Issa "threw a temper tantrum" while trying to late-board an Air France flight, creating an international incident. During the recall period, he made many menacing phone calls to Scott Barnett, a co-founder of Republicans Against the Recall.

Issa had a history of brandishing firearms when under stress, or to make a point to his employees, or to "send a message" to business rivals. In many ways, Darrell Issa embodied the inchoate anger roiling under the $3 million homes and manicured gardens and SUVs maintained by that part of California that perceived itself to be in crisis. He belonged to that top tenth percentile income bracket that saw its future eradicated by "taxes," by the issuance of driver's licenses to the people who tended their gardens and mopped their floors and blew fallen leaves off their lawns, by affirmative action, by bilingual education, by wetbacks spilling over the border. Still, Darrell Issa had the whiff of rotten fish about him, a trace of some fetid glandular disorder or the stubborn lingering smell of the arriviste.

And then, once the recall petition was certified, and the special election scheduled, Issa suddenly decided not to run. He wasn't anyone's favorite cup of tea in the first place, but Arnold Schwarzenegger's entry as a candidate effectively removed whatever tiny possibility Issa might have had in the general fracas. The latter withdrew in what was tactfully reported as a "tearful announcement."

In an interview with *Inc.com*, a publication Issa had once awarded himself an imaginary prize from, the non-candidate put a game spin on the whole misadventure: "If you can take $1.7 million and leverage it against a $38 billion problem and help fix that problem, then it's the best leveraged capital you can invest."

Some would stipulate that that depended on whose $1.7 million and whose $38 billion Issa was talking about. He took the occasion to cloud his 1973 weapons arrest, the 1980 indictment, and other notable achievements of his own by attributing them to his brother, who was, he said, such an incorrigible car thief that he "even stole two of my cars." Issa spoke of this brother as a kind of evil twin whose messes he'd been cleaning up for years. "Had I at times been unwilling to implicate my brother in things that I knew or could have known that he did? Yeah."

Issa did, actually, have a brother. Witnesses had noticed singed hair on Issa's brother's arm the day after Joe Adkin's car alarm company burned down.

"One delightful thing about the movement to chuck Gray Davis out of office," declared Michael Lewis in the *New York Times* (September 28, 2003), "is that so many people in so little time have come to suspect they might be the next governor."

Over 500 people filed papers to run for governor, and 135 were finally certified and listed on the ballot. You could run simply by paying a $3,500 fee and submitting a petition with sixty-five valid voter signatures. You needed a California address and a phone number.

The state insurance commissioner, John Garamendi, dropped out of the race even before the filing deadline. He may have been the first to deplore the whole business as "a circus," which became a popular term of disapprobation. Coverage of the race tended to distinguish circus candidates, or geeks, from serious ones, suggesting that only a certain kind of person was what Garamendi considered capable of "serious contemplation of the fundamental reforms necessary to restore our government systems."

Impossible to know if Garamendi meant the kind of person who had helped California drop from the country's highest educational level to second from the bottom, or the kind of person who had instituted the original California university system, which guaranteed a college education to anyone who qualified for entry regardless of whether or not he or she could pay for it. The last of the latter kind of person hadn't occupied the position in question since Jerry Brown departed it in 1982.

What Garamendi seemed to mean was neither of these kinds of persons, but merely the kind of person who might plausibly become governor without turning the state over to another Ponzi scheme, as Pete Wilson, for example, had when deregulating the energy industry.

Lieutenant Governor Cruz Bustamante was that kind of person. So were Peter Ueberroth, Peter Camejo, and Arianna Huffington. Bill Simon Jr., who had previously lost an election to Gray Davis, was maybe that kind of person. Tom McClin-tock, though really not that kind of person at all, made it under the wire for no more discernible reason than that he was a pro-fessional politician.

Most of these candidates had enormous personal fortunes, and all were, in fact, in one sense or another, professional politi-cians, and the various factions supporting one or another of them were somewhat reluctant to view Arnold Schwarzenegger as that kind of person. When you got right down to it, Arnold Schwarzenegger wasn't even a person. Arnold Schwarzenegger was an image.

He was also a harbinger of the circus becoming the center instead of the periphery. The circus included a substantial cross section of California's professional classes. In terms of political experience, there was little to distinguish the other geeks from Arnold Schwarzenegger besides stardom, the access to power it provided, and his marriage to a vestigial Kennedy.

The circus referred to candidates whose supposed charac-terological deformity had something in common with the world from which Schwarzenegger had emanated, who were clearly expanding the market for their personal brands, whose ideas for "fundamental reforms" often had more specificity, if nothing else, than Schwarzenegger's own expediently shifting and weightless platform.

There was, in other words, a political class in danger of los-ing its hegemony, its ability to frame debate and define the pub-lic interest. The recall process had been conceived to disrupt the arrangements of exactly such a class, something nervously ac-knowledged by candidates like Cruz Bustamante, who gave at least token support to a "no on recall" vote and ran as if on a contingency basis.

As per the *NYT,* many people had "come to suspect they might become governor," though most of the 135 candidates knew perfectly well they would not. After the filing deadline, continual polling reflected shifting majorities for Cruz Busta-mante and Arnold Schwarzenegger, the other candidates polling in single digits. (The preliminary yes or no question ran consistently against Gray Davis.)

Most circus candidates were intent on "sending a message," like *Dharma & Greg* producer Bill Prady, who ran "to make the whole thing seem ridiculous," and Ron Palmieri, a gay candidate "running to make the point that everyone else running is an ignorant fool." Ned Roscoe, a libertarian owner of smoke shops, ran on behalf of cigarette smokers. Reva Renz, a bar owner, wanted to abolish alcohol taxes. I, frankly, would have voted for either of the latter two.

Kurt E. "Tachikaze" Rightmyer, a middleweight sumo wrestler and Pushcart Poetry Prize nominee, offered a mixed platform of tighter border controls, tax relief for small businesses, and "complete decentralization of government."

Rich Gosse, "America's foremost spokesman for singles," campaigned on a "Fairness for Singles Platform," pledging not to accept "a dime of special interest money." Gosse himself was no longer single, having met his wife, Debby, at a singles party, but vowed to "continue to work full-time serving singles."

Candidate Larry Flynt, whose *Hustler* empire had branched into legal gambling, opposed the recall, and simply wanted the press to consider his ideas and perhaps bring some free publicity to the recently launched Hustler Casino in Gardena, the Southland's home of card clubs and other such enterprises. Flynt's chief revenue-producing idea was to introduce slots into private casinos, which he believed would generate enough tax money to balance the budget.

Gary Coleman, the troubled former child star of a long-ago television sitcom called *Diff'rent Strokes,* ran because the *East Bay Express* asked him to. Signatures for Coleman's ballot petition were gathered entirely at an Oakland A's game.

Mary Carey, star of *5 Guy Cream Pie, Grand Opening, Tit Happens,* and other adult movie features, proposed taxation of breast implants and a "Porn for Pistols" exchange program to get handguns off the streets, and promised to wire live Web cams into the governor's mansion.

And finally, there was Angelyne.

The mainstream media offered fringe candidates and their messages as comic sideshow acts, but prolonged scrutiny of the recall phenomenon opened a slightly different perspective. The glancing moment in which a heterogeneous range of voices became audible in the political process, and their instantaneous marginalization, illustrated how poorly the political system apprehended ordinary people—and how differently "ordinariness" was conceived by political culture and the popular culture.

"Serious" candidates represented credible ideologies and proposed changes that were understood to be infinitely negotiable, if not impossible, and expressed intentions, desires, attitudes, and wishes that sounded like every mushmouthed political rhetoric anyone had heard in eons, except for Arianna Huffington and Peter Camejo, who really did articulate a systemic and intelligent overhaul of the entire system, in Huffington's case starting with the revision of Proposition 13, which had set California on an inevitable course to crash-and-burn-land, despite intermittent South Sea bubbles like the high-tech boom and aerospace industries, back in the late seventies.

The "message" geeks were merely the parodic form of "serious" politicians, who "stayed on message," or veered off message, tried on issues and discarded them until one seemed to resonate—quite often, one that was weirdly irrelevant to the general welfare.

Angelyne personified irrelevance. A breasty blonde of indeterminate age who advertised herself on billboards, Angelyne had absolutely nothing to say, no message whatsoever to send. Since the early 1980s, Angelyne had refined celebrity to its narrowest, emptiest definition. People "knew" about Angelyne, and some even, apparently, imagined they had "a personal relationship" with her, simply because she had posted gigantic billboards of her own image where no one could avoid seeing them—on Sunset Strip, for example.

Who she was, what she was, and what she ever hoped to be were the kinds of empty questions Angelyne had inspired in numberless vacant minds since her earliest manifestations.

Sightings of the flesh-and-blood Angelyne, if indeed that is what she is, dating back as far as 1996 are posted on a Web site called The L.A. Grim Society. Some are strictly factual, such as "Sunday, March 18, 1996 (5:33 pm)—ANGELYNE SIGHTED—Driving northbound on Pacific Coast Highway at Rambla Pacific in her pink Corvette." Surprisingly many are starstruck. However, the overwhelming majority of these postings are hostile.

"This past week at Long's Drug in the Beverly Connection. Her pink 'vette was parked outside . . . I think she was waiting for a prescription (viagra, gin, and a blindfold—for her date, no doubt). She looked positively unreal—about 70, with huge breasts and huge hair and huge make-up that had little to do with her actual facial features . . . I missed her exit, but the clerk at the cosmetics counter by the door was visibly aghast at the apparition. Why I am not a pillar of salt, I don't know."

The bill of particulars against Governor Gray Davis left the personal odium attached to him unmentioned, but beyond the petition page, it slipped uncontrollably into news coverage.

Mayor Willie Brown of San Francisco candidly noted that Davis had *no friends*. Davis's neighbors, interviewed in Sacramento, couldn't wait for him to vacate the governor's mansion.

"That man is like paste," one told the *New York Times*. "Like gray paste. Not one ounce of charisma there. I thought you had to have charisma to raise money. How the hell does he raise all that money?"

The answer to this particular question was not especially appetizing, as many Californians had become aware. Reporting a Davis campaign appearance in early October 2003, a *Los Angeles Times* correspondent referred to Davis as "aloof, cautious, condescending and emotionally stunted." Hardly uninflected reporting, but nevertheless the most tersely accurate description of the man himself.

Davis had risen in the Democratic Party ranks in the obdurate, imagination-free manner of most of the country's career politicians. He exemplified the empty suit that moves ahead by showing up, like a party hack from the old Soviet Politburo.

He had nothing tangible to recommend him. He appeared to have been deposited in the public sphere by the laws of entropy. After working for Tom Bradley's 1973 mayoral campaign in Los Angeles, Davis became Jerry Brown's chief of staff in Sacramento. He then won a state assembly seat in 1982, and later, the state controller's job. He lost a Senate race to Diane Feinstein in 1992—a race in which Davis's vicious campaigning methods, as per Schwarzenegger's accurate phrase, "puke politics," were widely deplored. In 1994, he won as lieutenant governor, a party-affiliation-autonomous position, in the same election in which Republican Pete Wilson won a second term.

Davis ran his first race for governor against Dan Lungren, the state's attorney general, winning in that uniquely contemporary phenomenon, the "technical landslide"—Lungren, in other words, was such an unpalatably right-wing crackpot that Davis triumphed as the blander of two evils. He incarnated Joseph Conrad's flabby, nondescript, mediocre, and unexceptional devil, in effect, as opposed to one more virulent and overtly destructive. Davis's second win, against Simon, was even narrower than George W. Bush's first actual one (if, in fact, the latter wasn't rigged just enough to avoid a repeat of the first mess, which had spoiled the national appetite for electoral litigation and recounts, in any case, for decades to come), with far smaller voter turnout and approval numbers roughly half of what he'd started out with.

Like certain New Democrats of the Clinton kind, Davis cobbled together a makeshift constituency by selling out parts of the traditional Democratic base—from which it had moved so far to the right it could no longer be considered the Democratic base, anyway—while co-opting bits and pieces of the neoconservative agenda.

In practice, this translated into brainless support for the death penalty as a capricious, class-based option, the "three strikes you're out" statute, and a lavish pandering to the prison guards union, which empowered such fanatical, medieval entities as the Victim's Rights Movement and Mothers Against Drunk Driving. (In this area, as in several others, Governor Schwarzenegger has pantomimed an illusory repudiation of the status quo, being the first California governor since Jerry Brown to endorse the parole system as it was designed to function, rather than interpreting the theft of a pizza slice by a twice-convicted felon as grounds for life imprisonment. Indeed, Governor Schwarzenegger has granted parole to more prisoners in one and a half years in office than all California governors since Jerry Brown, Democrat or Republican, combined. I believe this has less to do with "liberal" conviction than expedience: a serious fracas has been brewing for some years between the prison guards union and the corporations exploiting California's draconian sentencing laws. The union has long seen an advantage in incarcerating as many people as possible, resulting in the construction of prisons becoming one of California's few remaining growth industries. The corporations who've been building new prisons all over the state wish ultimately to operate them with their own, non-unionized staff, as a privatized entity. Schwarzenegger's relief of prison overcrowding is designed to postpone this impending dogfight until the already grossly unpopular Department of Corrections becomes too weak to flex its muscles in Sacramento.

Unlike the extortionate, corrupt prison guards union, an entirely sensible, four-and-a-half-month strike of supermarket workers at Vons, Albertson's, and Ralph's, provoked by the announcement that forty new Wal-Marts were opening in California, was settled in February 2004 on less than satisfactory terms for workers, in part because public solidarity with working people had quickly exhausted its own patience. (Wal-Mart itself, vis-à-vis its treatment of employees, is reportedly sued more often than any American entity besides the U.S. government.)

Consider how far we have come from the New Deal: the *Japan Times,* in a November 14, 2004, article on ResFest, a touring short film festival arriving that month at LaForet Museum in Harajuku, lamented the obstacles Jason Wishow encountered while shooting "his all-vegetable, stop action rendition" of *Oedipus* during the supermarket strike. "Imagine having to explain that you need to cross a picket line because a scene you're shooting requires 'a taller onion,'" the director quipped. (Even my father, a staunch atheist who worked in Roosevelt's CCC during his youth, informed me many times that I would go to Hell if I ever crossed a picket line for any reason whatsoever.) The notion that the making of a film is of some transcendent importance in the world of non–make-believe human beings is merely a symptom of a culture of contempt.

Appeasement of the contempt culture, for Gray Davis, meant holding positions antagonistic to people you would later have to depend on—people who valued public service at least as much as personal ambition. Like Clinton, Davis came into office with a party majority in both legislative houses and alienated it—through bad strategy in Clinton's case, in Davis's by vetoing most progressive legislation proposed by his own party.

Davis never made useful alliances. His entire career was littered with fundraising improprieties and sweetheart deals with corporations and habitual extortion from unions. He was pay-to-play without any charm or rhetorical garni. There were elegant methods for doing these things, but Davis never learned them. He was cursed with the personality of a constipated pallbearer and deaf to all natural allies.

As Issa's Rescue California pumped steam into the recall drive, Davis desperately sought a claque of his own. Taxpayers Against the Recall sprang into existence, bankrolled by Davis's customary shakedown victims, designed to siphon manpower from the state's largest signature-gathering companies and run interference with the pro-recall petitioners stationed in strip malls and supermarket parking lots and at surface road intersections. After that fizzled, Davis made a belated attempt to appear human, accessible, and humbled by his mistakes, but continued exuding an air of entitlement and indignation at his increasingly apparent fate, like something feral with its leg in a trap.

The Democratic Party's heavy hitters, including Al Gore, Jesse Jackson, and Bubba himself, were roped into the fray, sooner or later, to chant encomiums to Davis. Even Diane Feinstein, who had scotched her own contemplated run for the governorship when Schwarzenegger announced his candidacy, found herself having to defend the odious Davis, though she looked rather more dignified about it than John McCain did while endorsing his own bête noir at the Republican Convention.

First A.M.E. Church in Watts was, as usual, the location of preference, the very heart of the party's long-abandoned base, but the claque, or anti-claque, brought no bounce at all in Davis's approval rating.

It was easier for the Democratic Party's charismatics to oppose the recall on a philosophical or paralegal basis than out of any real solidarity with Davis qua Davis. They spoke of a flagrant refusal to accept the result of a legitimate election. They mentioned chicanery of the sort that had tilted the Florida outcome in 2000.

A different governor might have weathered all this, since California's most dramatic problems had not originated with Davis, and he had attempted to solve them, with mixed results, though his solutions brought other problems—there were legitimate reasons, not all of them having to do with "gross mismanagement," why rolling blackouts and astronomical utility bills had hit Californians in early 2001, why the state budget was in the crapper, why the car registration fees were raised, and so on.

Unpopular personalities generate impatience. Especially in a crisis. While the severity of the California crisis was itself a debatable point, a feeling of crisis had squatted over the country at large for a long time. After the September 11, 2001, suicide bombings of New York and Washington, a court-appointed president of the United States had declared the nation "at war," not with any specific sovereign country, or several countries (though he had identified an "axis of evil" with rotational spokes), but with "terror," a routine practice of the United States itself, using the word to define an inchoate menace that was everywhere and nowhere, demonstrably ineradicable if diminishable until the end of time, hence a pretext for permanent war, never-ending crisis, and perpetually manipulable anxiety.

The malaise following 9/11—our very own Reichstag Fire—had different meanings for different people, but the sense of the world outside the United States as generally welcoming to Americans disappeared within months of an entirely opposite and equally unjustified condition of worldwide sympathy. Countries the United States had itself terrorized for generations expressed horror at the 9/11 events, perhaps proof that the hu-

man race is, on the whole, better than its most militarily powerful fraction. The militarization of public speech, an overall in-
citement to view the country as an embattled fortress, not only
nullified this manifest good will from abroad; it also created an
absurdly magnified impression of vulnerability among Americans, with a corresponding, irrational conviction that the world's
complexities could be settled by threats and blunt force, an ever-
popular recrudescence of savagery that has never enjoyed a very
long run in Western civilization.

The 9/11 attacks gave a pathetically inadequate, monocular
federal administration the opportunity to push through its neo-
feudal agenda of social control and Gilded Age economics,
heightening insecurities and driving the nation into irreversible
debt. Against such an alarming backdrop, California's ailments
fairly screamed for panaceas that didn't require too much analysis
and debate, since both practices had degenerated into sound bites
in the political arena. To the bewildered and traumatized who
continued to imagine that "fascism" described a condition other
than the merger of the state with corporate capitalism, *hasta la
vista, baby* sounded like as workable a program as anything else.
Other proposals contained too many actual words and often
sounded unpleasantly complicated. On the neocon side, Tom
McClintock attacked "waste," as if the American Empire hadn't
been built, precisely, on waste; contrarily, Cruz Bustamante proposed $7.2 billion in tax increases on tobacco and alcohol, a truly
idiotic program guaranteed to backfire—within months of the
draconic anti-smoking laws passed statewide, every bar and restaurant in Los Angeles, and no doubt everywhere else, had found an
effective way around them in order to avoid bankruptcy—along
with $4.5 billion in nebulous spending cuts. Peter Ueberroth, the

Olympic Games czar, nominally an Independent, advocated a 5 percent spending cut across the board, whichever board was in play. (This was never obvious in California to begin with.) Peter Camejo planned to raise income taxes on the top bracket by 1 percent. Not enough, but not bad. Arianna Huffington, by far the most articulate and intelligent candidate, and the most prominent one with no chance of winning, made a logical argument for curbing corporate tax breaks and the spiraling prison budget. An unthinkably sensible plan.

In the course of three September debates that included all the major candidates except Schwarzenegger, who was far too smart to argue with people more intelligent than himself (truly vast popularity in America is most frequently enjoyed by consumer products, entertainments, and personalities best characterized as "smart for the stupid"—a demonstrative flair for Pavlovian cunning rather than intelligence), only Huffington had the temerity to say that Proposition 13 had something important to do with the budget deficit.

The most obvious and equitable place to draw revenue is the property tax. But the United States is ruled, as Gore Vidal pointed out long ago, by two wings of the Property Party. Proposition 13 had frozen pre–Prop. 13 property tax rates in California at a pre-diluvian minimum. This was so apparent to anyone not owning vast property, and to many who did, or/and running for public office, that even Schwarzenegger's economic advisor, the investment billionaire Warren Buffett, briefly wandered off the reservation in mid-August to inform the press that, as a source of incredulity to himself, he, Buffett, paid $2,264 annual property tax on his $4 million house in California, as opposed to $14,401 on a $500,000 property he owned in Omaha.

Some outside observers considered the idea of the California economy in free fall a gross exaggeration. Paul Krugman, one of four or five remaining credible columnists for the *New York Times,* ridiculed Schwarzenegger's assertion that Californians were overtaxed from the minute they got out of bed in the morning. Another *Times* piece, filed after the recall election, cited a brisk housing market in California, a boom in military contracts, and a less than spectacular jobless rate. Californians, it said, "were used to their state routinely outstripping the nation economically," and hence experienced a less than vibrant situation as a catastrophe.

This was true, but also not true for entirely different reasons. Californians, like other Americans, are subliminally aware that the vibrant situation the United States has been in since the conclusion of World War II is itself a catastrophe of consumption, though the repression of this knowledge is the dirty secret we have all shared, without openly expressing it, for decades.

In the more immediate sense, unemployment in California did surpass the national average in 2003 by several ticks, as did the loss of manufacturing jobs. The technology sector alone lost 100,000 jobs between 2001 and 2002. The glass was either a little less than half full or slightly more than half empty. It didn't help matters that one of Gray Davis's pet unions, the prison guards, squeezed the state for a 35 percent pay raise when school spending and social programs were being razed to pay for the state's electricity.

It is surely an unusual American achievement that one of every 140 residents of the United States is incarcerated. This percentage easily tops that of such "failing states" as Côte d'Ivoire or

Sierra Leone. The United States far exceeds the incarceration rate of its nearest ideological enemy, Cuba, whose criminal population largely migrated to Florida decades ago, where it now works closely with our state and federal government.

California is, in this respect, well in the vanguard of the national culture. Its parolee recidivism rate is 40 percent higher than in any other state, mainly because the California Correctional Peace Officers Association (CCPOA) has lobbied against virtually any rehabilitative measures such as job training and education for the state's prisoners. It maintains brutal conditions in the thirty-two state prisons it controls, including lockdowns of racial groups, routine beatings, and intimidation. Several of its facilities maintain a lethal perimeter fence to save the cost of manning guard towers.

Davis granted an absurdly unmerited 34 percent salary increase, five-year raises with extra vacation time, shorter hours, and close-to-full-pay retirement at age fifty to the prison guards union. The union had exercised a grotesque influence on every California governor and legislature since Deukmejian succeeded Jerry Brown in 1982. Between 1980 and 2000, the state's incarcerated population jumped from 23,264 to 160,846, thanks largely to CCPOA's status as the most powerful lobbying entity in Sacramento. The union has promoted "three strikes" and other grossly totalitarian laws to ensure longer sentences for anyone jailed for anything. As of 2000, over 4,000 Californians had been sentenced to life imprisonment for nonviolent crimes under the three strikes law.

This has resulted in a booming prison construction industry. Private corporations—Cornell Corrections, Corrections Corporation of America, and Wackenhut Corrections—have built most of California's prisons. There were thirteen in 1985; by 1995, there were thirty-one. Naturally, the union's own success has brought it into direct conflict with corporations seeking not simply to build prisons but to run them as privatized industries.

The California Department of Corrections' annual operating budget was $923 million in 1985. The CCPOA's current annual budget is $5.3 billion. Today a California prison guard, occupying one of 20,000 jobs requiring no more education than a GED, within six years of employment is paid as much as a University of California professor. As Jill Stewart, a former *New York Times* correspondent, noted in a January 23, 2003, Web column, *iCapital Punishment,* Davis awarded the prison guards their incredible raise while his budget cuts of the same year snipped away "state funding for diabetic syringes for the low-income," among other threads of the social safety net. The prison guards union promptly wrote Davis a campaign check for $251,000.

The most enduring item in the prison guards union's rich legacy has been its influence in ensuring that almost all California judges appointed since 1982 have been tapped from district attorneys' offices. A judiciary drawn entirely from law enforcement has resulted in a perverse distortion of normally reversible judicial and prosecutorial malfeasance (the withholding of exculpatory evidence from defense lawyers, illegal police searches, admission of hearsay, etc.) into the so-called harmless error doctrine. This "harmless error" absurdity has been used to deny appeals and retrials in capital cases as well as misdemeanors.

It would be pleasant to think Governor Schwarzenegger's recent proposals to close certain prisons and cut the state corrections budget emanate from humane concern for those locked

away unfairly and brutalized by the ruinously over-rewarded ig-
noramuses who guard them, who often make higher salaries than
their supervisors—supervisors who are, in any case, prohibited
from questioning their faked overtime and abuse of sick leave.
But the question persists: what sort of rehabilitation will be offered people who may, at last, get paroled in a reasonable amount
of time, but have 55 percent deducted from any money sent
them from family members and friends, are taxed heavily on the
collect-only phone calls they're allowed to make, and now have
Arnold's signature to thank for rescinding their smoking privileges, while the Governator himself has erected a smoking tent
outside his smoke-free office building?

As governor, Schwarzenegger rejected clemency for a death
row prisoner who was seeking further DNA testing to excul-
pate himself in four murders in San Bernardino County committed twenty years earlier. Schwarzenegger doesn't need
campaign donations from the CCPOA, of course, but he may
well want some from Wackenhut Corrections or Corrections
Corporation of America, since all but five of the state's prison
facilities were constructed by private contractors and—who
knows?—maybe privatizing those is really what he has in mind.
It's expensive to pay as much as $100K a year to some yokel
with a taser gun when a trained "consultant," à la Iraq, can do
the same thing for much less chump.

FIVE

Schwarzenegger announced at the outset that he wouldn't take campaign money from "special interests." Indeed, he did refuse contributions from the California Correctional Peace Officers Association, against which public sentiment has been running ever higher for several years, and which has in recent times fallen under federal oversight for mismanagement and corruption. The term "special interests" is another strangely meaningless phrase that colors the political sphere as something unnatural—the pursuit of one kind of interest is held by another kind of interest as "special" in a pejorative sense, as if anything except rule by fiat, and certainly the democratic process, fell miserably short of adequate to these "special" times.

The notion that the "right" kind of "strong leader" is all the government a dazed and confused rabble needs to awaken itself to more enlightened "values" is a standard premise in many of Schwarzenegger's films. The paradigmatic one is the rather underappreciated Paul Michael Glaser film *The Running Man*, which presciently identifies television as an appliance used by a cynically powerful few to hypnotize the many, and quite scarily shows how simple it is for a "reality" constructed from images to be altered by technocrats and computer experts.

"The Running Man" is a game show that's weirdly conflated with reality itself—anticipating such brilliant conceptions as "reality TV," and much like a slightly more lethal tweak on the survival-on-an-uninhabited-island ones so marvelously acted that its one-dimensional contestants seem as real as the person next door. The film's equation of what people see on television with their perception of reality is explained in one of those rolling written prologues that so often precede movies set in the future: reality is more or less the same type of devastated and impoverished reality that Laurence Fishburne reveals to Keanu Reeves in the original version of *The Matrix*: that is, so intolerable that human beings are attached to biomechanical organisms that fill their heads with a virtual world full of modern goodies.

Like *The Matrix*, and like Schwarzenegger's *Total Recall*, *The Running Man* is set in an illusory world, and as in the "real" futures of the *Terminator* films, a small band of resistance fighters knows the truth and hopes to overthrow the regime of virtuality and domination by servomechanisms. In all these films, only one—The One, as Reeves is discovered to be in the *Matrix* films—has the preternatural power to "lead the resistance" to victory.

In *Total Recall* and *The Running Man*, Schwarzenegger is that indispensable leader, awakened from a false implanted memory in the former film, cop-turned-resistance-leader in the latter. The striking difference between these two films is the virulent anti-intellectualism *The Running Man* overtly suggests as the singular superior quality of the savior-leader Schwarzenegger: while the brainy, computer-whiz resistance has a plan to intercept the satellite feed of "The Running Man" that will preempt its propaganda with "the truth," Arnold, who doesn't know a computer code from a can opener, wins the day with a few antique Kalishnikovs and parts of the resistance willing to step up to the plate and shoot their way into the network's headquarters.

The incarnation of totalitarian evil in *The Running Man* is a seasoned game show huckster played by Richard Dawson. He is, by the way, nothing but a product salesman. The "Department of Justice" he works hand in glove with never makes an appearance in *The Running Man*—in effect, the *image* of power is "the enemy," totalitarianism's ventriloquial doll, rather than power itself. And the disposal of Dawson down the chute his show's "contestants" are dropped into to "play the game" of being annihilated by variously specialized "stalkers" is the culminating triumph of Schwarzenegger's "leadership."

It's at least worth a footnote that the last of these stalkers, Captain Freedom, is an out-of-shape former champ in the field who refuses to use the unfair gimmickry of wardrobe-as-technological-weaponry (his own long-retired costume is, in any case, falling apart) and storms out of the network control room when informed that he won't be allowed to stalk Schwarzenegger and his followers using only his natural strength; his refusal to submit causes his own execution, digitally simulated with the techniques of a special effects lab into a broadcast of Captain Freedom overpowering Schwarzenegger and impaling him on an Iron Maiden–like retaining wall. Only Captain Freedom has the integrity to wage an honest contest;

he's played in *The Running Man* by wrestling champion Jesse Ventura, who had previously appeared with Schwarzenegger in *Predator*.

The Running Man was released in 1987, the year Ventura retired from wrestling for health reasons—namely, complications from his exposure to Agent Orange as a Navy SEAL during four years of active duty in Vietnam. After a brief stint as co-host, with Gorilla Monsoon, of *Prime Time Wrestling*, and a subsequent job as commentator on *World Champion Wrestling*, Ventura became the mayor of Brooklyn Park, Minnesota, that state's sixth largest city, from 1991 to 1995. In 1998, running as the Reform Party candidate in the Minnesota gubernatorial election, Ventura beat the major party candidates, Republican Norm Coleman, the mayor of St. Paul, and the Democratic attorney general of Minnesota, Hubert H. Humphrey III.

Ventura served as governor for one term, from January 1999 to January 2003. He did not seek a second term, which he would certainly have won. In office, Ventura supported light-rail public transportation (the alternative to gasoline consumption implemented in the European Union), the medical use of marijuana, property tax reform, gay rights, and abortion rights. He didn't simply give these things lip service but passed legislation to advance these causes.

When the Reform Party chose Pat Buchanan as its presidential candidate in 2000, Ventura left the party, calling it "hopelessly dysfunctional." He is now closely aligned with the Independence Party of Minnesota.

Among Ventura's many positive qualities is his absolute candor and eschewal of the kind of political rhetoric Schwarzenegger, a "maverick" who ran as a Republican, routinely expresses in blunt, abbreviated sloganeering, only slightly less predictable in its actual wording than the tape-recorded "messages" political candidates of both parties bring to "debates" and public speeches. This "message-driven" rhetoric is routinely used to deflect any real dialogue or consecutive ideas from entering any debate, as Schwarzenegger so copiously illustrated in the one recall candidates' debate he deigned to participate in (with questions screened in advance by his advisors).

Among other things, Ventura openly admitted visiting prostitutes before his marriage, and stated that prostitution should be legalized. He also declared in a *Playboy* interview, "Organized religion is a sham and a crutch for weak-minded people who need strength in numbers. It tells people to go out and stick their noses in other people's business." He vetoed a bill to promote the recitation of the Pledge of Allegiance in public schools. He visited Cuba on a trade mission in 2002, and subsequently denounced U.S. sanctions against Cuba.

Known as Jesse "The Body" Ventura in his World Wrestling Federation days, Ventura engaged in a "sport" no more "sporting" than Schwarzenegger's bodybuilding competitions, but pure show biz, which Ventura also candidly admitted. The World Wrestling Federation does indeed stage wrestling contests without fixed outcomes, but the theatrical aspects of its offerings are far more important than whether any particular wrestler wins or loses—there are "evil" characters among its ever-changing cast, and "good" ones, presenting themselves as stereotypes, much like the "stalkers" of *The Running Man*. ("The Body," by the way, had been an "evil" WWF star.)

Ventura accomplished many good things in Minnesota, where his single term in office is positively remembered, even by citizens who voted against him. In 2004 Ventura endorsed John Kerry's presidential candidacy.

It was even less probable that a former WWF star would win a gubernatorial election than that a gigantically famous and popular film star would. Ventura had, of course, first had some actual experience in government as a city mayor, a job that is not as honorary in Minnesota as it is, say, in those Californian micro-cities where Clint Eastwood and other movie stars have occasionally held mayoral jobs. And Ventura exceeded anyone's expectations: he was entirely honest and dedicated to the public good. He said exactly what he thought without calculating the political consequences in advance, particularly in denouncing organized religion.

Schwarzenegger, in contrast, even had to calculate the only moment in which he could possibly have become governor of California—calculation is, after all, his foremost skill. Only in a specially scheduled recall election could Schwarzenegger run without any formal nomination by the Republican Party, in such a shortened campaign period that it effectively eliminated any time for voters to reflect upon the actual personhood and life history of Arnold Schwarzenegger instead of simply adoring his film image and voting for the hero of every action movie that more or less everyone had seen in theaters or on television (in the East, and certainly in California, Schwarzenegger's films were shown virtually every day and every night on one or another network or cable channel, often two different films on different channels at the same time), and only in a moment of artificially inflated "crisis" that was well on its way to at least partial resolution during Davis's second term. In the special election, voters expressed their disdain for Davis, and their general disappointment with the Democrats, "sending a message" to the party that so often claimed to represent them and routinely betrayed them to win elections.

The only sure-fire method of ensuring that California's energy stayed privatized and beholden to Texas corporations, which any reflection at all would have revealed as a disaster precipitated by Pete Wilson, was Davis's removal from office within the time limits for special elections stipulated by the recall statute. Former governor Wilson and his "team," of course, were Schwarzenegger's closest advisors. And as soon as Schwarzenegger became governor, Davis's policy of deregulating the state's utility suppliers once again became the state's policy. Just as the advocates of deregulation and "supply-side" economics invariably blame the catastrophes and inequality they inflict on ordinary Americans on the failure of their ideological enemies to let the right-wing experiment go all the way; eventually, perhaps over several centuries, some of the wealth concentrated among 1 percent of the American population would indeed trickle down to the peasants—enough, surely, to at least pay their burial expenses after they die from environmental poisoning or work-related accidents at uninspected, de-unionized manufacturing and other facilities. Or while serving a life sentence for a fender-bender in a Ralph's parking lot.

Schwarzenegger would almost certainly have failed to get nominated by his own political party in a regularly scheduled election, and even if he had, he definitely would have lost, since the Davis administration, despite its myriad distasteful aspects, had already begun to repair some of the systemic damage inflicted by the prior Republican governors, Deukmejian and Wilson, especially in the area of energy policy. The 2 percent rise in car registration fees implemented by Wilson's own legislative agenda might have been either eliminated or proven to serve the public interest, though only those who owned a Humvee or a Maserati were likely to find the expense inconvenient enough to cast a vote on the basis of it, and only the Republicans among them.

Apart from those suffering from what Thomas Frank, in *What's the Matter with Kansas?*, describes as a syndrome of deflected resentment impelling people to vote against their best interests, the poor, who really were hit hard by the increase, would have had trouble voting for Schwarzenegger in a regular election had they realized how much of his program—never particularized in his speeches, but available on an Internet Web site—was, in effect, Pete Wilson's program.

Even before the implementation of the next scheduled 2 percent increase in car registration fees, California had found it necessary to beef up its diminished DMV and police budgets by drastically lowering the blood alcohol level required for a DUI arrest (unless you're an attorney like F. Lee Bailey, who can afford to hire a lawyer like Johnny Cochran to dispute the breath or blood testing required *to avoid automatic incarceration*—basically a form of physical prior restraint, akin to the state censoring a newspaper article before publication—a DUI charge is more or less an automatic conviction ensuring several thousand dollars in windfall profit for the state, promotion of police officers via quota systems, etc.) and by setting up entrapment zones around intersections where stop signs and other metal traffic warnings were either so vandalized or ill-sited that they were invisible to most drivers.

In his first term, Davis had had to compromise with the out-of-state energy suppliers empowered by the Wilson administration. At the outset of his second term, Davis supported Lieutenant Governor Bustamante's lawsuit against Enron and other companies that had blackmailed the state by staging rolling blackouts and creating "crises," and rejected a bogus offer from the energy pirates for payback equivalent to two cents on the dollar for all the money looted from the state of California.

The energy crisis of 2001 had actually begun in 1996, when California deregulated electricity. This "landmark legislation" was a direct result of more than $1.8 million in campaign contributions, to seven legislators, from the state's three private utilities, Southern California Edison, Pacific Gas & Electric, and San Diego Gas & Electric.

Deregulation was supposedly intended to allow utilities to buy power in a competitive market, resulting in lower consumer costs. After deregulation, the three utilities sold their power plants to eight energy companies: AES, Dynergy, Reliant Energy, Thermo Ecotek, Duke Energy, NRG Energy, Southern Energy, and Calpine. With the exception of Calpine, all these companies were incorporated in Texas.

The legislation froze utility rates at their highest historical level, 40 percent higher than the national average. Competition never materialized. The utilities began surcharging ratepayers for their own bad debts. By 1999, SDG&E had effectively regulated its retail market and could charge consumers whatever it wished to.

Wholesale costs rose as much as 3,000 percent during parts of 2000. Early in 2001, the Public Utilities Commission hiked consumer rates by 10 percent. Southern California Edison defaulted on $596 million in debt to out-of-state energy suppliers. The rolling blackouts started in Northern California. Emergency legislation in 2001 put the Department of Water Resources in charge of buying power for the state. It then empowered the state to sign long-term contracts "to meet the shortfall of electricity." The blackouts immediately ceased.

A second wave of rolling blackouts in March 2001 ended just as abruptly, after payments were guaranteed to small independent energy companies. The Public Utilities Commission imposed another consumer rate hike of 40 percent. PG&E filed for bankruptcy. Governor Davis issued a memorandum of understanding that Southern California Edison customers would pay Edison's debts. Edison's transmission lines would be transferred to the state. In May 2001, another wave of blackouts hit California, this time concluding when the state announced a $13.4 billion bond issue to finance its energy purchases.

If this sequence of events sounds opaque, the procedures for buying and selling electrical power were deliberately so after deregulation. There was a spot market with the volatility of IPO trades, speculation by third parties like Enron, and a secret buyup of energy chits by employees of the Department of Water Resources.

After eighty years of regulated electricity rates, deregulation produced a massive increase in consumer costs. The reasons given for this were specious, to say the least. It was, for example, argued that demand had surged, when peak demand, in 2000, was actually lower than in 1999, and never exceeded the generating capacity of California's own power plants. During the blackouts, demand for electricity was actually 10 percent lower than it had been in previous years when no blackouts occurred.

A study by the Foundation for Taxpayer and Consumer

Rights (HOAX: How Deregulation Let the Power Industry Steal $71 Billion from California, January 17, 2002) concluded that "at the visible height of the 'crisis'—the days of rolling blackouts—California's demand for electricity did not approach the state's capacity to supply it, or even, for that matter, the peak demand of previous days, weeks or years, when prices were relatively low and supply entirely stable."

Another incessant theme of the recall proponents was the lack of new power plants. In reality, 170 new power plants had been built during the 1990s. According to the California Independent System Operator, owners of unregulated plants started shutting down their facilities for maintenance in October 2000 "at a rate unparalled in previous years." It was, in fact, a 246 percent increase over the previous year, and, in 2001, 348 percent over that. The power companies simply took their plants offline to spike the cost of power on the spot market from hour to hour. When supplies tightened, energy trading companies like Enron bid prices up.

Several early studies concluded that the energy crisis was entirely mythical, but hard evidence of criminal manipulation didn't surface until the state had been overcharged $9 billion. Eventually it came to light that companies like Enron had institutionalized the art of gouging the California energy market. The scams even had names: Fat Boy, Death Star, Get Shorty.

Davis's gross mismanagement of the problem seems indisputable. But the separation of cause and effect encouraged by many of Davis's opponents, including Schwarzenegger, allowed the astonishing argument that deregulation hadn't gone far enough—an argument Social Darwinists had been making for years at the national level, envisioning a society where "kill or be killed" would logically replace the notion of communal responsibility.

In 2002, Lieutenant Governor Cruz Bustamante launched a private lawsuit to recover the pilfered $9 billion under the Unfair Business Practices Act. As it happened, wattage laundering and other fraudulent practices did leave a paper trail. There was even an audio trail, a tape recording of two Enron energy traders, as per the following dialogue (CBSNEWS.com, June 1, 2004):

If you took down the steamer, how long would it take to get back up?

Oh, it's not something you want to just be turning on and off every hour. Let's put it that way.

Well, why don't you just go ahead and shut her down.

They're fucking taking all the money back from you guys? All the money you guys stole from those poor grandmothers in California?

Yeah, grandma Millie, man.

Yeah, now she wants her fucking money back for all the power you've charged right up, jammed right up her ass for fucking $250 a megawatt hour.

It also happened that the Federal Energy Regulatory Commission (FERC), chaired by Patrick Henry Wood III (a Bush crony who had previously headed the Public Utility Commission of Texas, and a pal of Enron's Ken Lay), proposed to settle the Bustamante lawsuit for two cents on the dollar. This required the unlikely agreement of the Davis administration.

It may have been here, rather than in the brainpan of Ted Costa, that the recall idea really originated—and here, some have suggested, that Arnold Schwarzenegger entered the recall picture.

On May 17, 2001, Schwarzenegger met with Kenneth Lay of Enron and Michael Milken at the Peninsula Hotel in Los Angeles. Details of this meeting are sparse, but the mere fact of it is significant, in light of the energy program Schwarzenegger proposed during his campaign, to wit: "Create a working wholesale power market based on the lessons from other states and the FERC standard market design." "Affirm the commitment to private power by dismantling the California Power Authority." In effect, the Terminator was offering, as a solution, the free market model that caused the crisis in the first place, a model that caused Enron itself to crash a few months after Schwarzenegger's meeting with Lay. By December, Enron share prices had dropped from $95 to $1.

The difference between the circus of yesteryear and the circus of today is litigation. Frivolous tort litigation does not account for the absence of a national health system or the high price of prescription drugs. It does account for why we have Disneyland instead of Coney Island. We might like to have amusement parks as libidinally unbuttoned, as Freudian, as defiant of moral prudery as Coney Island, but thanks to personal injury lawsuits (and our appalling subservience to convention), we have Disneyland, a place where nothing bad can happen to you and nothing really thrilling, either.

In the realm of electoral politics, litigation decided the outcome of the 2000 presidential contest, which had been clouded by balloting and voter registration list irregularities that would keep the mechanics of the voting process enmeshed in lawsuits for years into the future.

Lawsuits against the California recall were numerous, and at least two had considerable merit: *Davis v. Shelley* cited the use, in several counties, of punch-card ballots, and the consolidation of polling places, as violations of equal protection rights; *Juan Oliverez, et al. v. State of California, et al.* claimed that Monterey needed approval to change ballot procedures; in these cases, the Justice Department essentially ruled in favor of consolidation, and against challenges to the method of balloting.

The most significant case was brought by the ACLU of Southern California, with ACLU Northern California, ACLU San Diego, and ACLU Imperial County, again citing punch-card balloting in minority communities. On August 20, 2003, the ACLU complaint for injunctive and declaratory relief was rejected by U.S. District Court Judge Stephen V. Wilson. On August 27, an appeal filed in the U.S. Ninth District was accepted. On September 15, a three-judge panel reversed the original ruling, declaring that obsolete voting machines would disenfranchise voters in six counties. An appeal of the appeal filed before the full Ninth Circuit panel resulted in another reversal on September 23, allowing the election to proceed on October 7.

The salient factor here, the quiddity, the strange false bottom of it all, was the Supreme Court decision in *Bush v. Gore*, which had taken the oxymoronic form of a legal ruling that claimed for itself an exemption from use as a precedent. *Bush v. Gore*, unlike any decision by any court in the history of American law, applied only to itself. The ACLU exactly followed the logic of *Bush v. Gore*, and the full Ninth Circuit "upheld" that part of the Supreme Court decision that intrinsically could not be upheld—that is, the part that excluded the decision itself from what was understood, until then, to be the history of law.

The press coverage of Schwarzenegger's campaign was overwhelmingly derisive, stressing either the actor's presumed obtusity and bad behavior, or an agenda of corporate puppethood. The London *Guardian* was typical in ridiculing Schwarzenegger's thick accent, his incomplete sentences, and "the fact that his father, Gustav, was a Nazi stormtrooper"—the Nazi thing, in this reading, was "a boil" that the star had "lanced" with "a tactful $5m donation to the Simon Wiesenthal Center." The donation, and the implication that Schwarzenegger made it to whitewash his background, had been the core of *Spy*'s 1991 article, which stressed the Wiesenthal Center's failure to supply the magazine with a copy of Gustav Schwarzenegger's Nazi Party membership card as evidence of something extremely sinister. Nazism figured in various ways for journalists: Arnold had, according to unnamed sources, enjoyed playing Hitler's speeches in his bodybuilding days, "admired" Hitler's leadership qualities, had made "positive remarks" about Hitler: even Gray Davis found the Nazi theme irresistible, citing the connection between Hitler and Arnold Schwarzenegger as evidence of the actor's unfitness to govern.

The *Guardian* also decried Arnold's "puffing a joint" in the re-released version of *Pumping Iron*, as well as some Arnold utterances from the same film—"I like them with black hair, with brown hair, with red hair, with big breasts, with little breasts, with a big ass, with a little ass."

The *Independent* declared that the recall provision "has been activated after more than 80 years of disuse"—the technical inaccuracy occurred in most out-of-state coverage—and claimed that Schwarzenegger's "personal take on the American Dream" was "that Adolf Hitler was admirable because he was a little guy who made it big."

Richard Blow, writing for TomPaine.commonsense, noted Arnold's shrewd use of entertainment shows like *Oprah*, *The Tonight Show with Jay Leno*, and *The Howard Stern Show*, "entertainment over substance"—Schwarzenegger had, for example, destroyed a car to symbolize his opposition to the car tax—and the candidate's efforts to quash "unflattering information."

Amy Goodman, on *Democracy Now!*, brought Wendy Leigh and her celebrity bio back into the mix, stating that "connections between the Schwarzenegger family and the Nazis have been known since the early 1990s"—though the connection, singular, offered no useful implications.

There were follow-ups, and implications galore, yet none of them appeared to resonate with the restive populace. Goodman also replayed a PKFK/Pacifica interview by Jerry Quickley with African American bodybuilder Robby Robinson, who recounted several occasions when Schwarzenegger exhibited "overt horrific racism," the first at a banquet after the Russ Warner Classic in San Jose:

JERRY QUICKLEY: Now, this encounter that happened in San Jose, the Russ Warner Classic, as I said there were seven or eight . . . of you bodybuilders that were invited to guest pose and all paid to appear and guest pose. After the show as I said there was a large banquet and many of you there, dancing, having a nice time [when] in walks Arnold. He starts shouting "down with the blacks—niggers this and blacks [that]"—and this proceeded for about ten minutes until everyone is dead silent more or less and you eventually just got up and walked out as opposed to furthering the scene. Is that a fair rendition?

Robinson corroborated that that is exactly what happened.

On another occasion, Robinson had demanded that he, a principal character, and other background characters be paid at least $100 per day while working on *Pumping Iron*. When the producers refused, they staged a walkout at Arnold Schwarzenegger's Santa Monica apartment:

ROBBY ROBINSON: And when they say they wasn't going to give us any money I got up and walked out. Everybody followed me out the door. . . . That time [Schwarzenegger] just said, "That nigger, that's the second time that that nigger walked out of my house."

[Finally,] they gave everybody $100. Everybody was happy about that. And then after we got back to the gym, first day of shooting they pull out contracts, which supposedly gave us $10,000. Those contract[s] were never paid. They left everybody hanging. At the same time I found out through a friend of mine that [Schwarzenegger] spent a million dollars to buy the movie up so that everything about the racism and [that] Hitler didn't kill enough Jews was taken out.

The derision continued up to and a little beyond the election—on Election Day itself, *Los Angeles Times* columnist Steve Lopez referred to Schwarzenegger as "Der Gropenfuhrer," ruefully concluding, "If you can trample your own campaign promises, avoid talking about fixes for the state's problems, drive a Hummer in smog city, get accused of pawing 15 women, and still captivate an electorate in which Democrats hold a huge advantage, you deserve to be governor. And the people deserve to have you."

This was, in its way, the most provocative statement about American democracy, "direct" or otherwise, that anyone could make. If the will to power had so distorted perception that the people, given a choice, would choose against their own interests, whatever calamity ensued couldn't be blamed on the failure of other candidates to effectively present an alternative, or on the press's failure to interest the people in a real analysis of issues, but rather on the people themselves.

When it came down to the wire, the press was as deeply mired in a confusion of cultures as the country itself, as disposed to offer entertainment over substance as Schwarzenegger was. In the final days before the election, the *Los Angeles Times* reported profusely on Schwarzenegger's history of sexual assault, framing a plethora of accusations in the language of scandal and victimhood that had become the rote vernacular of belated grievances.

Women who had spoken to the *Times* "described their surprise and discomfort when Schwarzenegger grabbed their breasts." One claimed he had "reached under her skirt and gripped her buttocks." Another had been groped in an elevator.

Still another had been "asked whether a certain sexual act had ever been performed on her."

"Yes, I have behaved badly sometimes. Yes, it is true that I was on rowdy movie sets and I have done things that were not right and I thought were playful," Schwarzenegger told a San Diego rally. "But now I recognize that I have offended people. And to those people I have offended, I want to say to them that I'm deeply sorry about that and I apologize because that's not what I tried to do."

The *Times* quickly uncovered three more women Schwarzenegger had allegedly undressed in front of, tongue-kissed, and fondled on the buttocks; this was followed by five others who reported being spanked, or grabbed by the breasts or buttocks without their consent. The stories were detailed, in the sense of anecdotal verisimilitude, and offensive enough—but offensive enough to whom was the real question.

The country had quite recently endured the spectacle of its chief executive being hounded into impeachment by an implacably smarmy, repulsive special prosecutor, via a perjury trap contrived around sexual behavior. While the *Times* later spun its coverage as part of its duty to inform the public, it clearly expected the groping charges to damage Arnold's prospects; when they didn't, the first response was to blame the public, or at least that part of the public thought to deserve odium. On October 5, 2003, the paper ran a story by Susan Faludi titled "Conan the Vulgarian," which plangently asked, "Why are so many not offended?"

In Faludi's view, those who were not offended were American men, the same ones who had been disgusted by Bill Clinton's consensual cigar trick with Monica Lewinsky. These men saw Clinton as "feminized" by his loss of control "to a series of women," for which he had been "essentially shamed like a fallen woman," whereas Schwarzenegger equated masculinity with the nonconsensual humiliation of women, thus winning the approval of the locker-room set. Sex wasn't the point of this type of groping and importunity; being in control was. Clinton had lost control. Schwarzenegger had asserted it, in the manner of a rapist.

Faludi assumed that whatever Schwarzenegger had actually done amounted to criminal assault. So did Green Party candidate Peter Camejo, who saw in the groping allegations the nation's pathologies writ large: "If he were a black man, he'd be in jail. If he was brown, he'd be in jail. If he were a poor white he'd be in jail. What does it tell us about our society that a rich white person can do the type of things that he's alleged to have done?"

The victims, here, had an assortment of reasons not to file complaints against Schwarzenegger five, ten, or twenty years previously. The episodes they recounted would not have landed Schwarzenegger in jail, and it took a particularly lingering sense of outrage to think so. It did not take an especially grandiose intelligence to understand that continuing to work in the film industry and filing charges against Arnold Schwarzenegger were utterly incompatible activities.

What might have been true was this: if Schwarzenegger hadn't been a celebrity, but Camejo's generic black, brown, or poor white man, his accusers might have landed him in jail, and Schwarzenegger was so accustomed to this kind of cheesy behavior that he'd forgotten any specific instances of it, exactly as he claimed.

The real inegality in gender relations weighed less in this instance than an aversion to the perception of hysterical puritanism that even Republicans often find more effective as a last resort than patriotism, as per George Bush I's characterization of *ressentiment* against "anyone, anywhere, who might be enjoying himself." This was, after all, an election in which Schwarzenegger was running against Larry Flynt and the star of *Tit Happens*, among others, an election in which a candidate's sexual escapades could function as publicity assets.

It was never clear while he ran for office what Arnold Schwarzenegger would actually do as governor, as he frequently said one thing and said the opposite a day or two later, a habit described by some as confusing and by others as refreshing evidence of his willingness to change his mind. During one year in office, he managed to do several things he'd promised to do, and failed to do several others, and changed his mind frequently, which prompted many Californians to conclude that he was doing an exceptionally good job, and others to conclude that business as usual was still being done in Sacramento.

Schwarzenegger succeeded, for instance, in floating a $15 billion bond issue that "solved" the deficit problem—leaving a $7 billion shortfall to the following year, which, depending on what figures you looked at, was 1 or 2 billion less than the previous shortfall. When the $105 billion budget hit the usual deadlock, the Governator, as he was sometimes called, referred to the legislature as "girlie men" in the course of a speech at a shopping mall. The fact that the budget issues resolved themselves soon afterward was widely, and erroneously, seen as evidence that the legislature had "folded," though the usual favors were traded and the usual compromises made.

He did, by fiat, rescind the car tax increase. The legislature blocked his proposals to cut funding for schools and social programs. He vetoed a bill legalizing the importation of prescription drugs from Canada. The legislature "banned cruise ships from dumping drainage from dishwashers, showers, laundries and wash basins within three miles from shore." He proposed, unofficially, to make the legislature part-time. They foiled his negotiations with the Pomo Indians to build one of the world's largest casinos in San Pablo. He set up a smoking tent on the grounds of his Sacramento office building.

SIX

Some final notes on the recall.

In the end, even many people who didn't feel any special animus against Gray Davis discovered that they disliked him intensely. "People got tired of me after a while," Davis himself concluded. Many whose political beliefs would seem to have ruled out Schwarzenegger as a plausible candidate found themselves voting for him.

As in many situations where the prospect of anarchy, even a little anarchy, offers itself as an alternative to boredom, the sheer exuberance of overturning the given carried the day, and, insofar as the special election reflected it, carried the state of California as well.

Throughout the recall period the notion of California as "the bellwether" of America found its way into think pieces. The Jarvis Amendment had been the bellwether of the Reagan tax revolution, for example. California term limits had been the bellwether of term limits elsewhere in the country. Schwarzenegger's victory, like Jesse Ventura's in Minnesota a few years earlier, struck newspaper columnists and assorted minions of Fox, MSNBC, and CNN as, indisputably, the bellwether of maverick politicians gaining the ascendancy. Farewell to politics as usual.

To which one could respond yes, and no, and maybe, in roughly the same breath. A situation where it was suddenly possible to speak of a "Kennedy Republican" was one in which the dynamics of American power were somehow seriously in flux. Yet congressional redistricting and an embedded bureaucracy of patronage guaranteed an essentially static power arrangement in Washington; moreover, the country was believed to be immutably "polarized" between left and right (despite the ownership of both sides of the divide by the same corporate lobbyists)—one "liberal" talk show pundit, exhorted by Cornel West to move beyond this binary paradigm, plaintively asked, "What else do we have?"

It's a desolating question. The implied absence of anything besides mutually exclusive ideological postures servicing different segments of the same business community evokes a society that's something less than a society, an aggregate of interchangeable antagonists rather than a community.

What Arnold Schwarzenegger represents in the dream life of the general population requires its own special elucidation. What he represented as a candidate was a cosmetic resolution of the right-left trope. On many social issues he was, is, considerably more "liberal" than any California governor since Jerry Brown, while his stance on economic questions thus far has been gratifying or at least palatable to conservatives, if not neoconservatives. Neither circumstance upsets the distribution of power.

Kennedy Republican or Rockefeller Democrat, Schwarzenegger is an emetic throwback to the time of cultural agnosticism, when the people who owned the country perceived a distinct advantage in leaving people's private business and cultural expression alone, in funding art they didn't understand or approve of, in giving at least nominal support to the right to dissent, keeping their attention fixed on the business of making money. They were happy to send the country's artistic avant-garde abroad, all expenses paid, as goodwill ambassadors, proof that the United States was more than a nation of philistine materialists and trailer park yahoos; their descendants, on the other hand, had recently withdrawn federal funds for the U.S. Pavilion at the Venice Biennale, after slashing the National Endowment for the Arts budget to a figure equivalent to the cost of Band-Aids on a single military base.

In Washington, it had become doctrinally taboo to recognize that both President Roosevelts had applied the brakes to corporate piracy and supported the rights of labor for rational, self-interested reasons rather than hatred of the rich or love for the working person; the Progressive movement and the New Deal materialized, in large part, out of the astute surmise that the have-nots could only be pushed so far before causing the patrician classes real trouble. At the national level, the concept of buying the good will of social progressives with the occasional legislative concession to civil rights and the First Amendment had evaporated with "the culture wars," in which one side located the soul of the country in James Brown and the other side in Pentecostal fanaticism. Schwarzenegger offered Californians the possibility of a mixed, secular bag of unimportantly progressive reforms and a state government inflected, to no real advantage to the powerless, with precisely the "Hollywood values" the religious right deplored as the work of Satan.

• • •

American intellectual pieties, which change seasonally, have managed to demonize the philosopher Jean-Paul Sartre for his political activism and his indisputably wrong decisions in certain political matters. Yet Sartre's thought remains vital for a secular world.

It is a sad commentary on the current valuation of the activity of thinking that the most conspicuous contemporary "expert" on Sartre's philosophy is the vapid fashion plate and inch-deep "philosopher" Bernard-Henri Levy. M. Levy was not the first public intellectual to win attention with his good looks, merely the first to hang onto public attention for decades because of his inflated, movie-star debut in the realm of popularized philosophy and the inflation of his pontifications and pretensions into thoughts most aptly characterized as "smart for the stupid."

It would be useful if academics and journalists alike would read, or reread, Horkheimer and Adorno's *Dialectic of Enlightenment* with a greater degree of skepticism than that to which a certain tendency of the Frankfurt School has been subjected since World War II. It was not the Enlightenment that paved a direct road to Auschwitz. Quite the contrary. It was the sleep of reason.

It would be well for those concerned for the resuscitation of American democracy from its present-day, painfully inadequate life-support systems to visit, or revisit, an essay by Sartre, the title of which would most accurately be translated as "Elections: A Trap for Assholes."

There were elections in the old Soviet Union, and "elections," per se, are as common a feature of dictatorships as they are of democracies. When they become a tawdry exercise in cynicism rather than a true reflection of the citizenry's informed decisions concerning its own welfare, and when election fraud simply amounts to a coin toss over which of two oppressive twins gets to siphon public money into the hands of his respective corporate owners, it's time to do something a bit more energetic than showing up to vote, even in a "special" election.

Why has America fallen victim to a prolonged amnesia about its own actions in the world, and why do its most belligerently reflexive champions believe that to show the body bags or coffins of those who've given their lives in this country's service is equivalent to treason by American mass media?

As an advocate of animal rights, I am as prone as anyone else to be heartened while reading a fairly derisive "Talk of the Town" item in *The New Yorker* (December 13, 2004) recording the fact that Arnold Schwarzenegger, as governor of California, signed into law a bill prohibiting the inhumane methods used to enlarge duck livers for the production of foie gras—a practice first exposed in visually explicit detail in Gualtiero Jacopetti and Franco Prosperi's 1962 film *Mondo Cane*.

Yet this also immediately brings to mind the following, from Hans Magnus Enzensberger's 1964 essay about the Eichmann trial in Jerusalem, "Reflections Before a Glass Cage":

Statute about the killing and keeping of live fish and other cold-blooded animals of January 14, 1936:

#2 (1) Crabs, lobsters, and other crustaceans whose meat is designed for human consumption are to be killed, if possible, by being tossed into strongly boiling water. It is prohibited to put the animals into cold or lukewarm water and bring the water to a boil afterwards.

Telex Berlin Nr. 234 404 of November 9, 1938, to
all Gestapo offices and headquarters:

1. VERY SHORTLY ACTIONS AGAINST JEWS,
PARTICULARLY AGAINST SYNAGOGUES, WILL
OCCUR IN ALL OF GERMANY, THESE ACTIONS
ARE NOT TO BE INTERFERED WITH. . . .
3. PREPARATIONS ARE TO BE MADE FOR
THE ARREST OF ROUGHLY 20 TO 30 THOU-
SAND JEWS IN THE REICH. PARTICULARLY
WEALTHY JEWS ARE TO BE SELECTED. FUR-
THER INSTRUCTIONS WILL FOLLOW THIS
NIGHT. . . .
GESTAPO II. SIGNED: MULLER.

I had the extraordinary fortune to be born an American
in the exact chronological center of the twentieth century. Of
the time when I came into the general non-narrative, the noble
historian Eric Hobsbawm has written:

A "chronology of major guerrilla wars" compiled in
the middle 1970s listed thirty-two since the end of the
Second World War. All but three (the Greek civil wars
of the late forties, the Cyprus struggle against Britain in
the 1950s and Ulster (1969–), were outside Europe and
North America . . . the list could easily have been prolonged. The image of revolution as emerging exclusively from the hills was not quite accurate. It
underestimated the role of Left-wing military coups,
which admittedly seemed implausible in Europe until a

dramatic example of the species occurred in Portugal in 1974, but which were common enough in the Islamic world and not unexpected in Latin America. The Bolivian revolution of 1952 was made by a conjunction of miners by a military regime in the late 1960s and 1970s. It also underestimated the revolutionary potential of old-fashioned urban mass actions, which was to be demonstrated by the Iranian revolution of 1979 and thereafter in Eastern Europe. However, in the third quarter of the century all eyes were on the guerrillas. Their tactics, moreover, were strongly propagated by ideologues of the radical Left, critical of Soviet policy. Mao Tse-tung (after his split with the U.S.S.R.) and, after 1959, Fidel Castro, or rather his comrade, the handsome and peripatetic Che Guevara (1928–67), inspired these activists. The Vietnamese communists, though by far the most formidable and successful practitioners of the guerrilla strategy, and internationally much admired for defeating both the French and the might of the U.S.A., did not encourage their admirers to take sides in the internecine ideological feuds of the Left." (Hobsbawm, *Age of Extremes,* New York: Viking Penguin, 1994, pp. 435–36)

I did not have the privilege of knowing Hannah Arendt. But I have had the luck to live in part of her time, and while I can never hope to possess a fraction of her brilliance, I can try, as anyone with any mindfulness at all can, to emulate her fearlessness in dark times. Along with such extraordinary figures as Mary McCarthy, Herbert Marcuse, Renata Adler, Susan Sontag,

Joan Didion, Frantz Fanon, Noam Chomsky, Howard Zinn, Gore Vidal, Edward Said, Arundhati Roy, James Baldwin, Hans Magnus Enzensberger, Alexander Kluge, Angela Davis, and so many others whom I consider, in Mary McCarthy's phrase, "the last of the tall timber," Arendt has set the bar of intellectual courage for my generation and those to come exceedingly high, not least by implanting in lesser intellects like my own such ineradicable habits of skepticism that, to quote Outkast, "we can't be amazed, even if you pull the pin on your hand grenade."

Arendt: "No one has ever doubted that truth and politics are on rather bad terms with each other, and no one, as far as I know, has ever counted truthfulness among the political virtues. Lies have always been regarded as necessary and justifiable tools not only of the politician's or the demagogue's but also of the statesman's trade. Why is that so?" (Hannah Arendt, *Between Past and Future: Eight Exercises in Political Thought*, 1977, pp. 227–64)

Arendt: "The question that imposed itself was: Could the activity of thinking as such, the habit of examining whatever happens to come to pass or to attract attention, regardless of results and specific content, could this activity be among the conditions that make men abstain from evil-doing or even actually 'condition' them against it? . . . And is not this hypothesis enforced by everything we know about conscience, namely, that a 'good conscience' is enjoyed as a rule only by really bad people, criminals and such, while only 'good people' are capable of having a bad conscience?" (*The Life of the Mind,* New York: Harcourt Brace Jovanovich, 1978, p. 5)

In the present moment of easy mass manipulation by invoking the supposedly inexplicable phenomenon of "terrorism," I like to remember that few intellectuals among the American cultural elite ever attempted to understand why Ulrike Meinhof abandoned a comfortable and accepted role within her own country's intellectual class to join the far less cerebrally gifted Andreas Baader and Gudrun Ensslin, along with Holger Meins and Jan-Karl Raspe, in the Red Army Faction of the 1970s.

Among the few public intellectuals of that time to seek a better answer than the received wisdom du jour were Jean-Paul Sartre, who risked his own exalted reputation to visit Andreas Baader in the special gulag constructed for the "terrorists" of the day, the infamous prison at Stammheim—a less viscerally punitive, but in certain important respects crueler, torture chamber than even Abu Ghraib—and Jean Genet, who had nothing to lose and the audacity to publish a central document of that era, the essay "Violence and Brutality," which Betsy Sussler and others who produced X Magazine in New York in the late 1970s had the intellectual integrity to print in translation.

It's often a self-protective and sanity-retaining habit to shrug off the insults of history with the usefully indifferent, indisputable phrase, "shit happens." It does indeed. But nothing happens for no reason, even if we do not know the laws of history and never will. In every tragic tango, there are two partners responsible for the degree of violence enacted by the dance. When Americans wake from the thanatological transports the thrill of the tango instills in its most overtly aggressive partner, perhaps the United States will stop repeating the same brutal dance I have witnessed throughout my lifetime, and its citizens will see the full ugliness of this spectacle rather than a display of peacock-like patriotic splendor. But we will have to learn how to distinguish a Hollywood movie from reality first, and learn the bitter lesson we have taught the rest of the world.

A Fulsome Assortment of
Acknowledgments

Much of this little book primarily derives from public documents, such as those issued by the Legislative Analyst's Office in Sacramento, which provides entirely apolitical, unopinionated summaries of, for example, Senate Bill 1223 (Chapter 102, Statutes of 2000), aka Proposition 34, regarding campaign contributions and expenditures; from transcripts of legislative hearings; from broadcasts and transcripts of the California gubernatorial debates and the Republican National Convention; from Web site postings of such documents as the August 23, 1971, memorandum to Mr. Eugene B. Sydor Jr., Chairman of the U.S. Chamber of Commerce's Education Committee, from Lewis F. Powell Jr., nominated three months later, and confirmed, as an associate justice on the United States Supreme Court; etc., etc.

While I consulted many sources to try sorting out the California energy crisis, the most statistically detailed and comprehensive account of it, from which one can see in understandable terms what the monthly surplus of wattage was between January and August 2001 (initial capacity plus new megawatts minus average off-line megawatts equals supply available, with figures for peak demand, surplus, and average spot market price per month, contrasted with average daily maximum temperatures in Sacramento, San Francisco, and Los Angeles), is authored by the Foundation for Taxpayer and Consumer Rights in Santa Monica; trickier things to pin down, such as energy contracts, corporate subcontracts, cut-out companies, middlepersons, facilitators, etc., involved following the usual endless trail of paper bread crumbs left in the wake of myriad corporate and private entrepreneurs—annual reports, discrepancies in statistical findings and tax declarations, etc., etc. The budget deficit was, if anything, an even murkier issue, and finding the right equation between collected revenues, disbursements to counties and cities, federal grants, the service budgets and consumption demands of various localities, and the fine print in legislature undercutting "estimates," however one tries to break it down, is still confusing enough to cloud a precise analysis, at least for someone as numerically challenged as I am. Here, too, public documents and statistical reports proved the best sources of a good guess—a better one, I like to suppose, than was widely asserted.

For all kinds of information, however, I am indebted to both reporters and opinion columnists, especially the staff of the *Los Angeles Times*—I can't possibly list all the relevant writers, but Gregg Jones, Peter Nicholas, Michael Finnegan, Doug Smith, Joel Rubin, Eric Slater, Zeke Minaya, Marisa Lagos, Janet Hook, Erica Werner, Rebecca Trounson, Nancy Vogel, Jennifer Warren, Jeff Leeds, James Bates, Sue Fox, Roy Rivenburg, Mark Z. Barabek, Matea Gold, Dan Morain, Melinda Fulmer, Scott Reckard, Ron White, David Zucchino, William Lobdell, Mai Tran, Melinda Fulmer, Tracey Weber, Megan Garvey, Carla Hall, and Jack Leonard were among those whose exhausting hard work and clear-headed writing I depended on, especially when

I happened not to be in California during parts of the period discussed in this book. Steve Lopez's columns, too, were especially useful in locating the real issues involved in the recall process. Patrick Jarreau and Eric Leser, correspondents for *Le Monde,* also kept me up to speed on day-to-day developments when I was not in L.A., as did the reporting in the *Guardian,* the *Independent,* and the *Sacramento Bee.*

I cite all these people and publications because they maintain a standard of integrity and understanding of the reporter's job— I include Steve Lopez, who writes opinion columns, because of his extraordinarily well-informed and honest appraisal of events and utterances, without filtering out what he doesn't want to hear—that is quickly vanishing from American news media.

No one who writes about California could even pretend not to be indebted to Mike Davis, whose intermittent analyses of the recall and its peculiarities in *TomDispatch* illuminated the complicating elements that so often create a smoke screen around matters of public concern. Davis's books, especially *City of Quartz,* are indispensable reading for anyone trying to understand California and Los Angeles, and many other things, too. Likewise, Joan Didion's *Where I Was From,* which appeared sometime during the second draft of this book, clarified many important issues of a kind I am slow to perceive.

Regarding California itself, there are far too many essential books important to the big picture to list them all, but the ones I consulted most compulsively while writing this book were Mark Arax and Rick Wartzman's *The King of California: J. G. Boswell and the Making of a Secret American Empire* and Mark Reisner's *Cadillac Desert* and *A Dangerous Place: California's Unsettling Fate,* along with Louis Adamic's *Dynamite: A Century of*

Class Violence in America, 1830–1930, Frank Norris's novel *The Octopus,* and Upton Sinclair's novel *Oil.*

If the reader wishes to connect a lot of dots fast, the most direct route would be to start with *Chapters of Erie* by Charles Francis Adams Jr. and Henry Adams, which remains the most astute and concise book ever written about American capitalism and its political reverberations, proceed to Norris and Sinclair, and go from there to Ted Nace's *Gangs of America: The Rise of Corporate Power and the Disabling of American Democracy* and Joel Bakan's *The Corporation: The Pathological Pursuit of Profit and Power.* The stories of the railroads in the Gilded Age, and their role in California's history, of the Southern Pacific's political dominance, which inspired Hiram Johnson's reforms, which in turn produced the California recall statute, and, at the same time, the grotesque empowerment of the American corporation evolving from the 1886 ruling in *Santa Clara County v. Southern Pacific Railroad,* are perhaps the key narrative lines, with all their stems and branches, accounting for what California, and the United States, have become more than a century later.

I also have Ann Louise Bardach's feature story in *Los Angeles Magazine,* "Taming the Hydra-Headed Carnivorous Beast," to thank for connecting the sudden boosterism for Schwarzenegger's candidacy in the tabloids to an anthrax attack in Florida. Jeffrey Rosen's book *The Naked Crowd: Reclaiming Security and Freedom in an Anxious Age,* provided an analytical model for charting the phenomenon of "personal branding" and "marketed authenticity" as exhibited in the recall campaign period.

Concerning post-9/11 America, *Bush v. Gore,* and other subjects referenced here, I am especially indebted to Renata Adler's *Irreparable Harm: The U.S. Supreme Court and the Decision*

That Made George W. Bush President and Mark Danner's *The Road to Illegitimacy: One Reporter's Travels Through the 2000 Florida Vote Recount.* Other important sources are the volume *Bush v. Gore,* which provides the texts of the successive court decisions that produced the results of the 2000 presidential election and a wealth of variegated interpretations, edited by E. J. Dionne Jr. and William Kristol; *The Vote: Bush, Gore and the Supreme Court,* edited by Cass R. Sunstein and Richard A. Epstein; *The Votes That Counted,* by Howard Gillman; *The Miami Herald Report,* by Martin Merzer and the staff of the Miami Herald; as well as David A. Kaplan's *The Accidental President,* Noam Chomsky's *9/11,* Joan Didion's *Fixed Ideas: America Since 9.11,* with a preface by Frank Rich, Jane Jacobs's *Dark Age Ahead,* and Elaine Cassel's *The War on Civil Liberties.* For the widest perspective on post-9/11 America, it's useful to read Curzio Malaparte's *Coup d'Etat: The Technique of Revolution* and, of course, Hannah Arendt's *The Origins of Totalitarianism.*

I must personally thank Rob White of the British Film Institute for his patience and understanding, as the writing of this book has delayed the completion of a long-promised one on Luis Bunuel's *Viridiana;* and my agent, Betsy Lerner, for extraordinary support in some hideous moments. I also thank Colin Robinson and The New Press for allowing me extra time to finish, and my editor, Amy Scholder, for her remarkable fortitude, invaluable advice, and persistent encouragement.

I also understand, finally, why acknowledgments in this kind of book often seem longer than the books themselves: there are far too many people to thank for so many things that I really have to say, as some authors habitually do, "You know who you are." But I must specifically thank Marie Baklayan, Jamie Vega, and the staff of the Highland Gardens Hotel; Wendy Brandow; Bob Brandow; Margo Leavin; Suzanne Fenn; Roger Trilling; Elena Ackel; Marilyn Holle; Steve Wasserman; Charles Rydell; Barbet Schroeder; Bulle Ogier; Bill Rice; Taylor Mead; Lucien; Michel Auder; Nicola Lanzenberg; Laura Cottingham; David Rimanelli; Glenn O'Brien; and Karen Finley, without whose invitation to become Nico Liza for an evening I might not have met, at least in such a frontal context, Jack Doroshow, aka Flawless Sabrina, and Michael Phipps.